CEREMONY

Aboriginal and Torres Strait Islander people are advised that this book contains the names of people who have passed away.

The stories in this book are shared with the permission of the original storytellers.

Praise for *Ceremony: All Our Yesterdays for Today* ...

'Wesley Enoch and Georgia Curran's interwoven personal stories powerfully affirm that ceremony is a living, breathing practice – something we have always done together as a people, Black, white or Brindle. Through ceremony, we come to understand the world and our place within it. It's how we connect: to each other, to Country, to our ancestors, and to those yet to come. As a Blackfulla, this book reminds me that despite the ongoing impacts of colonisation, we have always found ways to keep ceremony alive. And the river – the life force that ceremony connects us to – still flows. It flows through all of us, strong, unbroken, and eternal.'

—Dr Rachael Maza, AM

'So much to learn here. This is a compelling interweaving of reflections and dialogue between an anthropologist and a famous artistic director on a genre of activity so closely identified with Indigenous Australians – on continuity, adaptation, and concern for intergenerational transmission but also on 'ceremony's' association with the future as inspiration for protest, dance and theatre and for the future.'

—Professor Fred Myers

'A graceful meditation on how ceremony and ritual can nourish our lives – and a powerful testament to the wisdom of First Nations practices, offering deeper ways to understand the world and ourselves. Enoch and Curran draw from the deep well of First Nations knowledges to illuminate richer, more grounded ways of seeing, being and belonging.'

—Professor Larissa Behrendt, AO, FASSA, FAHA, FAAL

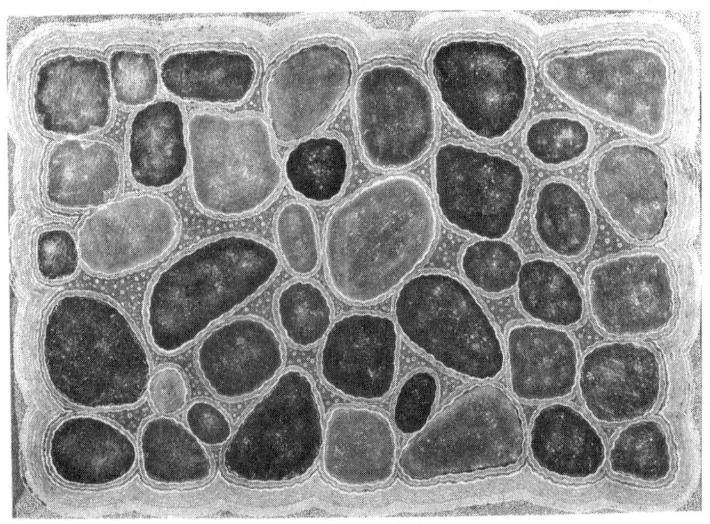

Danielle Gorogo, *Washpool Dreampool*, 2009

'The Washpool River is a revered gathering place. Every year, family and friends make the journey there to pay their respects to our Ancestors, honour our deep connection to Country and reaffirm the unwavering bond with Mother Earth. We gather there to partake in the smoking ceremony, one of the ceremonies that mark significant events – be they a Welcome to Country, a moment of mourning, or celebratory gatherings.'
—Danielle Gorogo

Danielle Gorogo is a Clarence Valley First Nations artist living in the Northern Rivers region, NSW. She is a direct descendent of the Dunghutti, Gumbaynggirr and Bundjalung nations. Danielle's multifaceted cultural heritage, which includes First Nations Australian, Papua New Guinean, Māori and Micronesian ancestry, is reflected in her art.

CEREMONY

All Our Yesterdays for Today

WESLEY ENOCH &
GEORGIA CURRAN

Thames
&Hudson

First published in Australia in 2025 by Thames & Hudson Australia
Wurundjeri Country, 132A Gwynne Street, Cremorne, Victoria 3121

28 27 26 25 5 4 3 2 1

ISBN 978-1-760-76407-4 (paperback)
ISBN 978-1-760-76428-9 (ebook)

A catalogue record for this book is available from the National Library of Australia

Front cover: *Washpool Dreampool* by Danielle Gorogo, 2009

Series editor: Margo Ngawa Neale
Cover design: Nada Backovic
Editor: Bernadette Foley
Typesetting: Megan Ellis

Printed and bound in Australia by McPherson's Printing Group

FSC® is dedicated to the promotion of responsible forest management worldwide. This book is made of material from FSC®-certified forests and other controlled sources.

Thames & Hudson Australia wishes to acknowledge that Aboriginal and Torres Strait Islander peoples are the first storytellers of this nation and the Traditional Custodians of the land on which we live and work. We acknowledge their continuing culture and pay respect to Elders past and present.

thamesandhudson.com.au

To all the Aboriginal Elders who have passed on to us their deep knowledges of ceremony and Country and brought to life all our yesterdays today.

To all generations yet to be born who will carry these ceremonies forward into the future.

NOTE ON STYLE AND SPELLING

The First Knowledges series seeks to honour the individual voices and stylistic preferences of each book's authors. Also, for different language groups, variant spellings occur for similar words, cultural groups or names.

NOTE ABOUT TERMS

The recently adopted collective term First Nations for Aboriginal and Torres Strait Islander people or the First Peoples of this country we now call Australia is a term borrowed from Indigenous peoples of America, and it comes with political undertones. This descriptor is not used by all Indigenous people of Australia, with some preferring to be called an Aboriginal person or a Torres Strait Islander person, others Indigenous, and yet others by their language groups. The concept of nations is viewed by some First Australians as a Western concept with imperial overtones. They prefer to be described as belonging to their clan, tribal or language group. In this series we use all the terms interchangeably.

NOTE FROM THE AUTHORS

This book is not intended to be a comprehensive overview of ceremony across First Nations Australia. There are hundreds of different Aboriginal and Torres Strait Islander groups that have various ceremonies and hold them for different reasons. It would be impossible for us to write about them all in this short book. We have taken a broad definition of ceremony but focus on examples that we are familiar with. We do not discuss any ceremonies that are secret sacred and intended for specific initiated audiences. We hope that the ceremonies we do discuss help readers to understand the many others that you may encounter.

CONTENTS

FIRST KNOWLEDGES

MARGO NGAWA NEALE, SERIES EDITOR

A person freshly returned from the Garma Festival in Arnhem Land some years ago lamented that us city Blacks have no ceremony. I retorted with: 'But we do! What do you think the smoking ceremonies one experiences at every public event are, if not ceremony?' Also, the Welcomes to Country, NAIDOC Week events, and performances by Bangarra Dance Theatre, such as *Kinship*, *Blak*, *Ochres* and *Knowledge Ground*, if not ceremony?

Our contemporary Aboriginal and Torres Strait Islander ceremonies cross time and place; from the Top End to the south coast; from centuries ago to contemporary times, all speak in varying degrees about ancestral connections to Country, identity, kinship and cultural values, regardless of their outward appearance and context. Whether it is a dance performance at the Sydney Opera House, a film, an Aboriginal awards night such as the Deadly Awards, or a traditional funerary, healing or initiation ceremony, the base purpose is invariably the same. Ceremonies, large or small, private or public, are repeated ritualised practices or sets of behaviours that teach successive generations about culture, law and society.

There are two broad categories of ceremony: a public, outward-facing set of ceremonies for outsiders from neighbouring clans or visitors, and a second set that are inwardly focused and include participating family and clan's people, without observers. These reaffirm identity and relationships while providing public displays of cultural power and competence. They are colloquially described as 'showing off' skills in an intergenerational transfer of knowledge.

This is in contrast to the public ceremonies that play to an audience with dramatic gestures and other theatrics. Both types of ceremonies are highly organised and deeply valued in a society richly laced with spiritual, cultural and ancestral beliefs. As Georgia Curran and Wesley Enoch, authors of this book, further explain, these ceremonies are 'dedicated to the building of cultural capital and social skill'. Every New Year I participate with my extended family and others in a smoking ceremony near Grafton on Country. There are rarely any observers; we all take part at various levels. As with so-called traditional ceremonies, there is an Elder owner (the custodian of the ceremony), a manager, helpers and participants depending to some degree on lineage and kinship ties. There are stories shared for cultural affirmation, respect for Country, Ancestors and the recently deceased with cross-generational transfer of knowledge. It is followed by feasting, fun and further bonding. We are urban or rural Aboriginal people who practice our past. Use of the term Makarrata, a peace-making ceremony held in Arnhem Land and popularised since it featured in the film *Ten Canoes*, has provided a new way forward for effective reconciliation among Indigenous and non-Indigenous Australians. It is now part of the national political language as a consequence of its use in the Uluṟu Statement from the Heart and during the Yes campaign for the Voice to Parliament referendum in 2023.

While ceremonies now come in many different forms – public festivals, intimate events, private and restricted occasions (with some being religious and others secular) – they must all adapt to change or disappear. To the outside observer they may look different, but their cultural purpose and intent remains the same or similar. We are an adaptive and dynamic culture that only survived millennia because our Old People had the capacity to change, exercise ingenuity and strong cultural purpose. As circumstances, context and place change over time, so do our practices. After observing one of many traditional Aboriginal ceremonies in Arnhem Land where I lived in the 1970s, I found out that what I thought was the Mosquito Dance was, in fact, the Aeroplane Dance. Arms outstretched, the dancers circled around while making a humming sound. The dance was explaining the Japanese bombing of Darwin (1942–43) in Yolŋu terms. This new content was embedded in the same structure and format and incorporated into a ceremonial repertoire to help make sense of a changing outside world. There are Barge dances, Buffalo dances and many more that enable people to explain the existence of new things.

You may be surprised to know that even the Garma Festival in Arnhem Land, considered to be the major cultural event of the year, has adapted many traditional ceremonies and dance forms, though they may still feel and look traditional. To accommodate the need to engage the whole country and not just the local clans for transfer of cultural knowledge, and to form bonds with politicians, celebrities and other Aboriginal communities, adaptation is critical. In addition to knowledge sharing and cultural exchange between related clans, Garma has also become political. It is a national forum for conferencing ideas and concerns, lobbying politicians and creating action plans.

Garma has also found ways to accommodate whitefella's ceremonies, such as the Australia Day Honours awards. In 2009 a performance was created to enable the family of a recently deceased person to receive that person's Australia Day Honour from the attendant Administrator of the Northern Territory. Wesley writes about this vividly in Chapter 5.

One need look no further than the 2000 Sydney Olympics to see an epic adaptive ceremony that was viewed by people around the world, and learn about who we are and where we come from. Like all ceremonies it spoke to our origin story, our national narratives and values while acknowledging Australia's ancient history. By putting Aboriginal and Torres Strait Islander people centre stage at the Olympic Games Opening Ceremony it also spoke to Australia's aspirations for First Australians. Hundreds of Aboriginal dancers were seen and dozens of different languages heard from across the country with men's and women's business in progress, a smoking ceremony, stilt walking Mimi spirits and the raising of the 35-metre tall Wandjina image, watched by some 3.7 billion people internationally.

Cross-generational expectations and interpretations between Elders and youngers can also bring on negotiated adaptions. Some Aṉangu Elders from the Central Desert region secured funding to participate in a desert bush weaving workshop. The young women really wanted to make the contorted anthropomorphic trees that feature in the *Seven Sisters* exhibition. However, the older women were deeply opposed because, they said, the trees in the Seven Sisters story were men's business, not women's business. The lustful male pursuer in the story shapeshifted into trees to lure the women to him when they needed shade or the delectable quandong fruit. Discussions between the women continued over several days. The younger women won out by arguing that there is no use in these old stories if they can't be relevant to now. What is their use if we can't learn from them? They went on to say that what they learnt was that if Wati Nyiru, the pursuer, can turn into a tree to trick the women, then so can we to trick him and hide. The older women were fearful of inviting harm for transgressing male business. Together they worked out some mitigation strategies to keep them safe and proceeded to complete the most stunning set of life-size woven trees, which became a destination installation in the global touring exhibition I curated with the mob, *Songlines: Tracking the Seven Sisters*.

Today we are all exposed in varying degrees to religious ceremonies such as Christmas, Easter, Diwali, Ramadan and Eid, Passover and Hanukkah, which are marked by holidays, feasts and certain rituals that are deeply rooted in the past. Then there are the more secular ceremonies such as ANZAC Day, King's Birthday and Australia Day (now shrouded in controversy, which Wesley unpacks in this book).

Rites of passages for the transition of married women into widowhood and readiness for re-marriage, current-day initiation ceremonies for boys in remote areas, and debutante balls for girls in cities and towns, have evolved new forms of expression in different parts of the country.

We all know to some extent where the religious and other ceremonies mentioned above come from, but where do the contemporary Aboriginal cultural practices and belief systems come from? What are their origins and purpose? This book and the series to which it belongs, is based on this fundamental enquiry. How do traditional practices and belief systems inform contemporary practices and beliefs? How is yesterday connected to today? The subtitle of this book – *All Our Yesterdays for Today* – beautifully captures this concept. As Wesley puts it, ceremony is a way of connecting all our yesterdays for today. He also challenges the use of the word 'traditions' when used as a static understanding of the past, rather than a dynamic process. Tradition is embodied in culture practised today, 'something that carries forward stories and values, not in a repeated, stagnant form but in creatively responsive ways to present-day contexts', as Georgia writes in Chapter 2. Neither are Easter and Christmas practised in the same way they were 100 or 200 years ago.

All cultures have ceremonies. It's universal. The Catholic Church, for example, also has its smoking ceremony – incense laced with frankincense and myrrh to purify a congregation just as our smoking ceremonies cleanse and purify. While there is a common humanity and need for ceremony in all cultures, there are some revealing differences between Australian Western/multicultural ceremonies and Indigenous ceremonies – a difference that essentially emanates from our relationship to Country. We view and experience Country as a personage, with whom we have a oneness and inseparability. It obliges us to nourish and look after Country as we would our mother, thus the expression Mother Earth. We are born into this distinct and existing relationship to the land, to flora and fauna, with inherited responsibilities.

Being an oral culture, our knowledge is passed on primarily through performance, with ceremony being the headline act. Ceremony is the crucible of all knowledge; it makes us human. Our non-text-based knowledge system needs to be retained and transmitted in an embodied form, which is the most enduring way of learning. It has allowed our people to live well and sustainably with each other and with Planet Earth for some 2000 generations, beyond any other cultural group on earth.

Indigenous culture expressed though ceremony is more focused on the body, in particular the body in place, in contrast to a focus on objects, as is the case in many aspects of Western culture. It is the physicality of doing ceremony as opposed to the materiality associated with objects used in ceremony. Lynne Kelly, author of *The Memory Code* and co-author of the first volume in this series, *Songlines: The Power and Promise*, makes the point that the human brain is hardwired to learn through song, dance, images and movement. One can remember an image or a song for a lifetime, but how long can you remember pages of text?

Material accoutrements such as clapsticks or rhythm sticks, feathers, ochres, bush-string dilly bags and painted surfaces are, by extension, ephemeral and therefore of transitory value. The practice of making is much more important than the final product. In the making, the maker talks to the object and sings its songs to breathe life into it, giving it form and purpose complete with personal and ancestral connections. During their use in ceremony these objects accrue cultural power. After the ceremony they lose their power and are reduced to residual traces of the ceremony, as described by the authors. This is unlike the status of Western ceremony, where objects are permanent and increase in value over time.

Today, however, our once-ephemeral objects have been incorporated into the Western system for display, and indeed a sophisticated new production stream for public consumption is well established, with Aboriginal art being the most prolific. Artefact is becoming art and art, artefact. This distinction is now blurred as they are both recognised by the dominant culture as holders of knowledge.

Attitudes to knowledge are the third notable difference between Indigenous and Western ceremony. In much of Western culture, access to knowledge is considered to be a right to be taken whenever and wherever without restriction, whereas in First Nations cultures knowledge is a privilege to be earned, something to work towards acquiring before certain things can be known. Knowledge is age graded and gendered. It is restricted by one's level of initiation, moiety and kinship classifications, and family lineage, which is different and more complex than the Western understanding of kinship as only biological. For example, knowledge remembered and regained on the *Seven Sisters Songline* project by the custodians that preceded the exhibition was deposited in Aṟa Irititja, an Aboriginal-managed archive. Unlike the Western library system, which is generally objective and democratic, Aṟa Irititja is subjective and restrictive.

Only those with inherited rights can access relevant knowledge. Wesley and Georgia talk of receiving rather than creating knowledge from relevant Ancestors.

Another critical difference is that in times past Indigenous ceremonies had no audience and many still don't. There were only participants, or soon-to-be participants such as those on the sidelines waiting for their part, or kids and young people in training, whereas in Western performative ceremony, audience is the focus. These more public performances can be seen as less ceremonial because they are not dependent on shared cultural values but function more as entertainment, or a diversion from life rather than didactic affirmations of life. But even the Western performance has its roots in ceremony.

Today some traditional ceremonies in remote regions are a fusion. Georgia writes in Chapter 8 about the community-focused contexts where observers watch the performance in a sectioned-off area and the singers and dancers engage with them through various innovative means. The lead dancer of Ngapa Dreaming, Nellie Nangala Wayne, found opportunities for innovation for ceremonies performed outside Warlpiri Country.

'Corroboree' is another term you may come across for ceremony. It was first coined to describe cultural performances by First Peoples for the pleasure of the colonists conducted during early encounters. Now they are more light-hearted community-based public ceremonies to 'have fun', as Georgia explains in Chapter 2, quoting Yamurna Napurrurla Oldfield.

This is the ninth book in the First Knowledges series. So hungry are people worldwide for knowledge and insights into contemporary

Indigenous societies that the original set of six books has now grown, with eight titles published already, plus some for younger readers. Like Songlines and ceremonies, the need for knowledge has a kind of circularity that may never end.

A fitting conclusion to my introduction is offered by Wesley and is worth repeating here. In the final chapter he examines the ceremony of truth-telling. He says that 'This country moves forward when we embrace ceremony', by taking all we 'have learnt from the past to find new ways of our history being alive today'. 'Maybe we need less politics, less campaigning where values and morals are traded for money and power' and 'more ceremony to come to terms with who we are and what we have done to be where we are, here and now'.

1

PERSONAL PERSPECTIVES

WESLEY ENOCH

I have never known ceremony the way my great-grandparents knew ceremony. I have grown up in a world of different privileges. A world where food was hunted in supermarkets and learning was presented to me in schools and universities, but that was not my only world. I also grew up knowing my family and where I came from. On a series of islands off the coast of Brisbane, on Quandamooka waterways and lands is where my story begins. Islands now called Stradbroke and Moreton are where I live now and where my grandfather's people are washed with the waves of the ocean, where grains of sand count out the number of people from countless generations. The islands Minjerribah and Mulgumpin have fed and housed my family for as many years as there are stories to tell.

We can go back thousands of years of fishing and hunting, of the running of the mullet and seasons of the dugong, the migration of the whales, the connection to the dolphins and the eugaries and oysters, crab and prawns. Thousands of years piled high in middens and buried deep in the sand.

Funerals are a ceremony with deep observance and commitment to sharing with others the memories of what has gone before, passing down from generation to generation ceremonies and rites that mark our culture. This story doesn't need to go back thousands of years – you need only go back just over ten years for the ceremony of the funeral of my father.

Aged sixty-five, my father died of lung cancer in 2014, and my family was prematurely thrust into the role of organisers for his funeral. There was a great deal of planning and negotiation, as all the different stakeholders in my father's life came to bear witness to his passing. His widow, uncles and aunts (my father was one of thirteen), cousins and friends, workmates and grandchildren, and us – his four children – were brought together over a two-week period of intense planning. Needless to say, there were tensions at times, with different people arguing for different observances and the constant need to reflect our contemporary lives.

In the few days leading up to the funeral my brothers, nephews and uncles and I attended to my father at the funeral home on the mainland – washing his body, shaving his face, combing his hair and dressing him. This was an intensely moving experience shared by this band of male family members in a ceremony of tears and care, a gentle preparation and personal farewell. Though we removed his wedding ring (something I now wear as a sign of responsibility to care for my mother), we dressed him in his football team colours – the Broncos.

On the day of the funeral my brothers and I woke at dawn to go to the gravesite on the island to be present for the digging of the grave. The story goes that my father dug the grave for my grandfather fifty years earlier. My grandfather died at the age of forty-three, years before I was born, and my seventeen-year-old father took a shovel and went to this same cemetery where we were standing now, surrounded by the bones of our forebears, to dig a grave. And though on this day we could only watch the backhoe digging up the sandy soil, we recounted this story our father had told us and recognised the need to be there when the earth was disturbed for his interment. In a way, to consecrate the ground.

My grandfather's grave is on top of the hill, surrounded by his sisters and other family. When I was growing up I always knew where he was buried because a huge gum tree acted as a marker. We would call it Grandad's tree, almost as if the tree was him – and in many ways it was. Over the decades, the tree has grown strong as it took the DNA and other nutrients from his body and drew them into its limbs and branches. I see this as a story of connection to Country. Imagine generation after generation buried in this land and how the trees and plants grow strong and feed the birds and insects that then feed many other animals or help spread the seeds across the landscape. Imagine how connected you feel to a place when the DNA of thousands of generations of your family have been transferred to the very ground you walk on. How deep and important that connection is.

After the digging of the grave, we then travelled by ferry to the mainland to meet the hearse, which was about to cross the Quandamooka waterways (Moreton Bay), bringing our father home to the island for the final time. As is customary, the ferry was full of mourners accompanying the body on this journey. There were farewells and family talks, hugs of greetings and sad moments as mourners held the hearse. When the ferry arrived at the island the mourners created a guard of honour for the hearse to travel the 500 metres to the community hall. My brothers and I walked with the hearse as it slowly moved up the hill. Never leaving our father's side along this journey home. Protecting him and accompanying him.

Inside the hall various eulogies were given and statements made, an Aboriginal flag draped over the casket, which had earlier been open for those who needed to say goodbye, and the protocols of family were followed, including the intergenerational carving up of duties. Grandchildren carrying the casket into the hall, the sons carrying the casket back to the hearse, and the brothers eventually taking the last short walk to the grave.

I will never forget the 400-strong congregation walking with the hearse from the hall to the cemetery, as with many funerals before it. At the front of the procession my cousins, brothers, uncles playing didge and clapsticks. Clapsticks that had been specially made for this funeral to help accompany the singing – this calling the Ancestors to take our father's spirit on this journey. The singing and music clearing the road and dispelling any bad spirits that might impede that journey. The men led the way, followed by the hearse. Behind the hearse the female relatives and then a long snaking line of vehicles that blocked the main street for at least 20 minutes.

At the grave side there were further words spoken and singing. When the time came for the burial the men produced shovels to fill in the grave. Shovels and spades passed around so that every male in the family, and some women, could add their contribution to returning the sand and soil to fill the hole. When this was completed and the sweat was mixed with tears, the women delivered the flowers and objects to adorn the grave. There is a tradition of making wreaths of native flowers from the island and many local trees were denuded so that the decoration of the grave could be complete. Then we took the clapsticks we had used for the singing and buried them in the soft ground around the grave for protection. Some cousins had brought sand from our grandmother's Country to add to the grave, mixing local sand with the sand from North Queensland, representing the mix of blood from different places that runs in our veins and can connect us to these different landscapes.

As is tradition on the island, uncles had collected coral and shell fragments to act as a final layer on top of the grave. This practice is recorded by anthropologists and early historians, but we know it goes back to long before the arrival of the colonists. Then we returned to the hall for sandwiches and tea, jelly slice and cake provided by family members and friends.

In the intervening year there was limited talk about my father. A practice observed to let the spirit travel without being called back to this place. In some families I know of the practice of not saying the deceased person's name. Also, I had removed several photographs of my father from public display in my office and home, again to ease the journey and avoid confusion.

A year later the family gathered again, this time to unveil my father's tombstone to mark the final stage of the mourning process. In some families this marks a return of the photographs from their exile and being able to talk about the person once more. A weekend of building a surround for the grave, removal of the brittle dead wreaths of native flowers and the rearranging of mementos – a piece of stone from the quarry my father used to work at, a metal frame of a kissing couple brought from downstairs in his den, a Superman button from one of the grandchildren, an empty circular picture frame made from three blue ceramic dolphins, a number of vases weighted down with stones and filled with brightly coloured plastic flowers to keep him company and tell anyone visiting that my father was highly respected and continues to be remembered. In addition to my father getting his tombstone unveiled, we closed a chapter and had a tombstone made up for my grandfather and his tree.

Funerals are a time of great importance to honour the deceased and for the bereaved family, and also an important sign of respect and continuity of cultural practice. Ceremonies connect us to each other and to the history of Country, a cultural obligation played out to mark the moment in time and connect to the age-old traditions. A rite of passage but also a teaching of the next generation. It is this repetition that marks it as ceremony as opposed to a one-off set of actions imagined for a single iteration.

Ceremonies can take many forms; in First Nations cultures it is the sense of intergenerational observance that connects us to our families, our Countries and our histories. Ceremonies are a way of connecting all our yesterdays to today.

GEORGIA CURRAN

There is no other way for me to begin my contribution to a book on First Nations knowledges than to acknowledge the extraordinary love, kindness, acceptance and enduring patience of the many First Nations people who have put up with me, looked after me, and insisted over time that I keep up my end of the intense work that living in a world centred on relationships requires. For the Warlpiri mob, with whom I have spent the most time living in Central Australia, it is ceremonies that hold their cultural worlds together. Over many years of 'doing business' with Warlpiri families, I have learned of their practical nature in that they set up a ritual pattern through which traditions, stories and relationships that give life meaning are carried into the future.

My upbringing in the 1980s in a rural part of the Gold Coast Hinterland (a place I know today to be Yugambeh Country) was one in which I engaged with few First Nations people. My parents did, however, perhaps quite unusually, ensure that my sister and I were surrounded by books of First Nations stories and histories. When I was born, I was even given an Aboriginal middle name, Kurita, from one of these books. My name comes from the story 'Wamili and the Waratah', about an expert hunter named Wamili, who loved collecting honey from the waratahs; Kurita was his wife. Unfortunately, as was often the case with these kinds of books published in that era, the Aboriginal group to which this story belongs was not acknowledged.[1]

Like many Australian school children in the 1980s and 1990s, my formalised education included little of Australia's First Nations history and culture. I do remember the whispers around the schoolyard one day during the heavily celebrated 'Bicentennial year', when my classmates and I arrived in the morning to find several wheely bins had been set alight beneath the grandly hung '1988' sign in our school's undercover play area. Though we were never told much about the politics behind these kinds of events, even as a kid I had a feeling that something wasn't right about the stories we were being taught about Australia's colonial history.

Due to my developing interest in different cultures and ways of life, I began studying anthropology at the University of Queensland and it opened up my world. My main lecturer, John Bradley, invited Yanyuwa women from Borroloola to our classroom each semester to teach about their songs, ceremonies, language and Country through participatory workshops, as was their way. Jackie Huggins, Michael Aird and other prominent First Nations people were our guest lecturers, sharing their perspectives and stories with us. My later years at university were also spent exploring grammars of Australian Aboriginal languages. In my Honours year I undertook a very bookish project focused on analysing documented word lists from languages spoken around the Gulf of Carpentaria – an exercise that revealed fascinating histories of movement and interactions of Aboriginal people in this region of Australia over a number of centuries. After I finished my undergraduate university years, I moved to the western New South Wales town of Bourke, where I worked for two years with Wangkumara language workers at the town's Aboriginal language centre. During these years, I visited the Country in south-west Queensland where Wangkumara people originally hailed from, before they were forcibly taken to a mission in Brewarrina, just to the east of Bourke, in the 1930s. The flooded rivers of the Channel Country prevented their attempted walk back and they ended up staying in Bourke. The last speaker of Wangkumara had passed away years before, but the excitement of re-learning this language and the evident joy and meaning this had in the lives of my co-workers was inspiring.

In 2005, I joined a research project alongside senior Warlpiri people from Yuendumu and three academics with long histories of working in the Central Desert, Nicolas Peterson, Mary Laughren and Stephen Wild. The aim of our project was to record and document Warlpiri Songlines, as Elders were becoming increasingly worried that younger generations were not learning these songs and the associated knowledge of Country, kin and ancestral stories. This was supported as an Australian Research Council Linkage project 'Warlpiri Songlines: Anthropological, Linguistic and Indigenous perspectives' (2005–2008), a partnership between the Australian National University, the University of Queensland, the Central Land Council and the Warlpiri Janganpa Association, which contributed funds from royalties it received for mining on Warlpiri Country. Warlpiri Elders had specifically co-designed this research project so that I could be involved as a PhD student living in Yuendumu, and contributed their own royalty monies especially so this could happen.

Soon after moving to Yuendumu I formed close friendships with Jeannie Nungarrayi Egan and her husband, Thomas Jangala Rice, who became co-investigators on the project. Jeannie was one of many incredible Warlpiri linguists central to the strong bilingual education program in Yuendumu, and has been well lauded for her contributions in this space. Her passion lay in documentation of language and culture, which is why she was so interested in driving the song recording and documentation project that I had come to Yuendumu to work on. When I arrived there, I was given the skin name Nungarrayi, meaning that Jeannie was my classificatory 'sister' – a connection that became important to everything we did together as it meant we had the same social positioning and related to others in the same way. As Jeannie's husband was a well-respected senior man this also gave us a unique opportunity to work with men, which I may not otherwise have had.

Jeannie tragically passed away in 2009 – a loss that was deep on so many levels. While travelling to Yuendumu for her funeral with my five-month-old baby, I thought about everything she never lived to see – she was excited that I was pregnant but never met my child, she had dedicated so much to our projects but never saw the outcomes. Jeannie's legacy lives on through memories of her and her input that is at the core of every part of my research since. My book *Sustaining Indigenous Songs* has a dedication: 'Ngajuku kapirdi-ki (for my big sister)'.[2]

During my first night in the Warlpiri community of Yuendumu, almost twenty years ago now, a group of elderly women invited me to come up to a cleared ceremony ground to the west of the community area. I soon learned that they planned to sing and dance until sunrise – for the last time formally mourning a much-loved senior woman who had passed away a few years earlier. Younger sister of the deceased, Peggy Nampijinpa Brown, now a dear friend and research collaborator, pulled me over to tell me what was going on. Like many Warlpiri women of her generation, Peggy loves sharing stories with newcomers to Warlpiri worlds and delights in those of us who honour these relationships across time. That night I sat with her on her swag as she whispered that a blue tongue lizard was very angry and wanted to burn his two evil sons. She kept emphasising that the lizard was going a long, long way south and reiterating that this was the story they would be dancing. Though I understood little at the time, over the years I learned more about this important Ngaliya Warlpiri story of Warlukurlangu Jukurrpa and its intimate link to the deceased woman and her sisters, many of whom danced that night.[3]

A group of around sixty senior women from Yuendumu and other nearby communities performed the ceremonial songs that she had owned and which had been 'closed' since her death, meaning they had not been performed for this period. This practice, similar to the one Wesley described above, when his father was not mentioned often following his death, allows the deceased's spirit, held in the songs, to return to Country in peace. The ceremonial event would mark the end of the period of closure and open up these songs again, so they could be performed for future generations.

As the sun began to set, creating the fuzzy light that I soon came to know typified desert evenings, I dragged my swag out of the car and joined it to one of the long rows of bedding, where many of the women had already gathered. Extraordinary beauty was all around me: the singing in unison by the group of women, the ochred designs on their breasts and upper arms, the dances and the power of and respect for the kuturu – two ritual poles standing in the centre of the cleared area. Their physicality also one with that of the focal Ancestors and the deceased woman.

This, my first taste of Warlpiri ceremony, was powerful! The ceremony was activating these long passed-on stories of Country and Ancestral Beings and their deep and intimate links with particular people and their kin. It was evident that vital cultural work was occurring. At sunrise, like many other all-night efforts, this one culminated in an intense exchange of blankets and other valued goods – an act that solidified prior and newly established relationships and ensured that Warlpiri families were entrenched in obligations to continue these ceremonies in the future. Despite the evident power of this ceremonial tradition, I couldn't help but also consider its fragility in the modern world – a tradition being held together by this small group of elderly women.

Over the years that have followed this first night in Yuendumu, I have participated in and travelled to attend many other ceremonial events across Central Australia. Some were of much grander scale and involved other community groups, and some quite intimate with individual families. As I worked in Yuendumu over these years recording and documenting many different genres of Warlpiri songs with various families, men and women, and different generations, my learning came to take a more analytical and formalised approach that was quite different from this participation in ceremonies. Yet during this time, Warlpiri people would often say to me in response to questions I had about various Songlines, stories and ceremonies: 'You know, you were there, and you danced!' My understandings of these events have taken a different form to most Warlpiri people who have been participating in these ceremonies since before they can remember, but some similarities do exist – understanding has to come slowly and cannot be rushed, and the only way to truly understand is through embodied participation.

The first book in the First Knowledges series, *Songlines* by Margo Ngawa Neale and Lynne Kelly, sets up the integrated knowledge systems of First Nations Songlines and the necessity of experiential engagement to properly understand – and the exhibition *Songlines: Tracking the Seven Sisters*, which Margo led, undertakes this on a virtual level. Like so many important cultural practices, it is the physicality of 'doing' ceremony that gives it its powerful social function and through which present-day people activate the timeless ancestral stories long held in Country.

2

WHAT IS CEREMONY?

WESLEY ENOCH

Where I come from we have a dance that calls the dolphins to help us as we're fishing.

When the mullet are running (a term to describe the mass migration of mullet) you can feel the change of temperature and how the season is shifting. The autumn months bring a time of feasting and gathering, a time when much business is done. Business could mean trade, rites of passage, family connection and certain ceremonies. In many ways, the word 'business' can mean any family, cultural or ceremonial activities in addition to the familiar ideas of 'buying and selling' through trade and barter. The abundance of food at this time of year could trigger a series of gatherings and exchanges for neighbouring clans, where marriages or rites of passage might be organised, and act as a reminder to sing certain songs and do particular dances. There is a dance that teaches us that through a deep, respectful relationship with the dolphin we can assist each other to survive.

The dance is simply the carrying of two sticks or spears out from the hip and moving them up and down to symbolise the slapping of the water. Slapping the water is a signal to the dolphins to come into the shore, and by doing so they drive fish into awaiting nets or to the shallows for spearing. When the dolphins chase them, some fish circle back after confronting the nets, so the dolphins can feast on them and the humans have the benefit of not needing to go out to the deeper water. This is a dance that teaches life skills and strengthens the connection with the dolphin; it is our ancestral totem and we view the dolphin as a family member.

Every culture has ceremonies. From the earliest establishment of family and clan structures, towns and communities, human beings have needed to find ways of remembering our history and passing on knowledge, to build a collective understanding of the changing world around us. There is something human in the need to connect with each other and share stories. Stories of where to hunt, lands that flood and the best places to find water in the dry, as well as stories of weddings or birthdays, which build connections and trust. Ceremonies help form deeper and stronger bonds between people in a community; in return, the greater the bond the more likely you are to rely on the community in hard times. Shared moments bind a culture together through generations and help build a social cohesion that is essential in times of threat.

A ceremony is a repeated set of behaviours that mark a remembrance of a moment in time or a transition from one state of being to another. Ceremonies are highly organised and deeply valued in a society, and may include ideas of spiritual, cultural, physical and social interactions. They can be handed down from generation to generation and remain relevant throughout time, uniting a diverse range of people from different backgrounds, social strata, demographics and ages. Ceremonies are dedicated to the building of cultural capital and social skill.

Language, song, dance, music and art are the cornerstones of most ceremony. The arts are the most effective way to create meaning in a society and the best way to make those moments memorable and repeatable. Teaching and transferring knowledge are done through the arts, as Lynne Kelly articulates in *Songlines: The Power and Promise.*[1] The human brain is hardwired to memorise what is learnt through images, song and dance, thus the success of our knowledge system over millennia. Through arts and cultural expression meaning is accrued and enduring.

Ceremony is not the exclusive property of First Nations people. Look around and you'll see that ceremony is everywhere. There is a series of religious ceremonies attached to Easter, Christmas, Diwali, Ramadan and Eid, Passover and Hanukkah, which are marked by holidays, feasts and certain rituals that may go back thousands of years. There are also civic ceremonies, which are in remembrance of an historic event or person, such as ANZAC Day, Labour

Day, Australia Day or a monarch's birthday, that draw you into a thoughtful, reflective mode. Sometimes through that remembrance we learn the lessons of history. There are ceremonies that mark a transition or provide a rite of passage; they include New Year's Eve (one year to the next), birthdays (from one age to another), Halloween (with roots in the act of communing with the dead), weddings (from single status to married with more social and familial responsibilities), graduations (rites of passage or initiation into more knowledge), christenings, B'nai Mitzvah, quinceañera, Ji Li and Guan Li and Seijin no Hi. Everyone has attended or participated in ceremonies, every family has them no matter how small or how big. First Nations Australians have ceremonies connected to the changing of the seasons, healing, initiation, diplomacy, hunting and connections to the creation of place.

There are many ceremonies that mark the changing of the seasons and a connection to place, such as the cherry blossom festivals in Japan, winter and summer solstice festivals from early religions, which mark the shortest and longest days of the year, and harvest festivals. Where I come from the Bunya Nut festivals celebrate an extraordinary abundance of these nuts and would bring people from all around for feasting and exchange. The running of the sea mullet, which happens mostly in the autumn months, would trigger a huge gathering of people to share in the bounty, trade and exchange stories. Each year the gatherings occur, and the ceremonies are shared and repeated. Repetition and reiteration are valuable tools for embedding ceremony in society.

THE LEARNING SPIRAL

I was taught by my Elders about a 'learning spiral' present in First Nations cultures, and how your role in a ceremony will change as you grow older, even when the ceremony stays the same. In many ways they were teaching me patience and to watch and learn rather than push to know things before I was ready. The spiral shows how you learn and pass on knowledge through the repetition. There is something comforting about things being repeated and completed and starting again, and with every repeat you become more familiar.

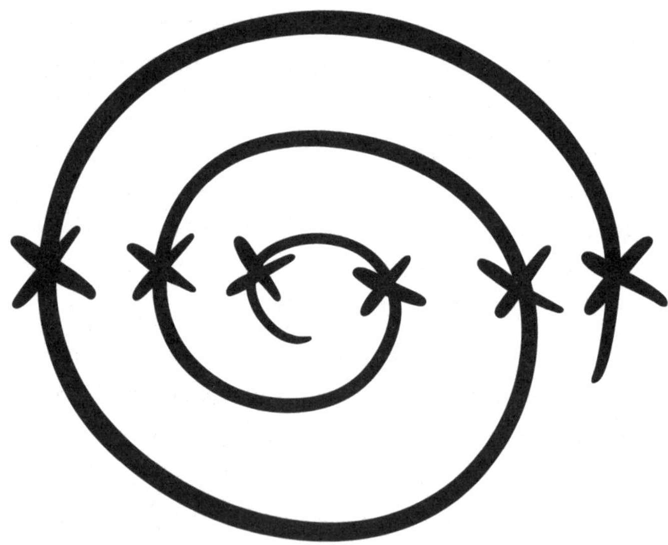

The learning spiral shows how your role in the ceremony changes as you grow older and learn more about it, and start to pass on that knowledge.

Think of it as a graduation process where, as a child you're cast as an observer and playfully engage in the ceremony from the edges. Those moments of cute kids doing the dance moves at the front of the main dance area where they watch and repeat; they're given permission to play and enjoy the attention they receive. Too often my attention is stolen away from the expertise and skill of the main dancers as I am captured by these young children and their sense of engaged play. As those children grow older they graduate to a serious learning mode, where the more experienced dancers help them to learn the dance and the spirit of the dance. They may be told to sit down and watch some more if they are not deemed to be doing it properly yet. The depth of dance may then be revealed as the child learns the story and song, the purpose of the dance and its literal meaning. At each iteration of the ceremony the young person is assessed before they progress to the next level of understanding. This process of watching and learning is not just for dance; painting, song, story all have the same notion of watching and learning through doing.

As you get older you may be encouraged to excel and grow strong in the dance, learn the metaphoric meanings behind it, not just the literal story of the creation of the mountain, river, island, animals and plants but graduate to learning the moral or values-based lesson in the story. Each time the dance is done, sometimes regularly, sometimes years apart, your role in it and your understanding of it grows. You develop your skills and understanding and the power of your dance reaches a pinnacle. Eventually, as a dancer, you are entrusted to teach the young ones. Then in older age you may become the keeper of the dance and have responsibilities to innovate, interpret the world and perhaps even create new dances for the clan to make sense of the world.

The dance may stay the same but as you grow the depth of your understanding of it increases and your role then is to keep it alive for the clan.

THE EPHEMERAL OBJECT

All cultures have ceremony. In many ways, Western cultures use objects to represent and celebrate ceremonies. Think of the Christmas tree, gift giving, the Easter egg, the crucifix, even the church or mosque, temple or shrine, the cenotaph, the statue, the tombstone, and birthday candles. I am not saying that First Nations cultures don't have objects (and there are some very powerful objects that should not be taken lightly, but these are not for me to talk about), rather that our ceremonies are defined by the body, the place and the practice of remembering. As a First Nations person being connected to the place you call home has many obligations. You find yourself engaged in the perpetually changing landscape and seasons and observing animals and plants.

Some objects used in First Nations ceremonies may have a sacred purpose for a moment and then they are discarded. Like the body or sand painting that is left to the elements to erase, the ceremony is ephemeral and time based; when it finishes it is left behind and recreated anew when it is needed. The practice of making is much more important than the end products of paintings, headwear, apparatus, leaves, feathers and skins. These are the residue of the ceremony, the remaining traces. The process of making these objects for use in ceremony does not give them greater importance over the doing of ceremony. It is a shame many Western institutions have collected and protected the objects of ceremony to act as the record of our cultures, rather than protecting the skills, knowledge and practice of ceremony. These collected objects represent a powerful but static rendition of our ceremonies, a memory of a moment in time but not necessarily of how it might be enacted in the future. This can also be said for anthropological records, video and audio recordings, where the Western idea of permanence supersedes the dynamic cultural practices of First Nations people. Ceremonies adapt and evolve through a process of reiteration. Though there is a strong sense of continuity, I remain concerned whenever the historical permanent record held in Western institutions is given greater value than the modern iteration of our cultural expression. I believe the skills of the people who created the objects and the knowledge of how they are to be used are more important to preserve than the objects themselves. This has changed a lot in the past few decades, but still, the holding of objects as the material proof remains a Western priority rather than a First Nations imperative.

SACRED AND SECRET SACRED CEREMONIES

There are sacred ceremonies that may be done publicly and 'performed' for anyone to see and then those referred to as secret sacred ceremonies, which are tightly held, and rarely enacted and for very special occasions. In this book we do not write about anything that is secret sacred. Everything we refer to is for public consumption. The difference between the public and the secret represents the kind of restrictions present in First Nations cultures – gender, age, family lines, skin group, geographic, initiated and many more. There are some ceremonies that are only for those who have gone through initiation and deemed culturally responsible to access the knowledge that accompanies them. Where much of Western culture views knowledge as a right, to be accessed whenever you want – for example, information on the internet where you can find out anything at the push of a button – in First Nations cultures we consider knowledge a privilege that must be worked for and earned. Just as in the learning spiral, you graduate to the next level of knowing when you show yourself worthy.

Ceremonies may sometimes overlap or coexist within a particular time. In the dance of the dolphin explained earlier, for example, the feasting and gathering could be a trigger for multiple things to occur or be organised – like a festival of different ceremonies happening through a singular time. There are small, inwardly focused, one-on-one ceremonies for healing, to arrange marriages or that are intended to make someone fall in love with you. While outwardly focused ceremonies are open to everyone to watch and participate in. Large-scale dance and song exchanges are held for the whole community and neighbouring clans. Elders might agree this is a time when a series of songs or a Songline that hasn't been seen and heard for a long time should be enacted.

A community may have a series of overlapping ceremonies, each being informed by the other. A widow who undertakes a healing ceremony before the arrangement of her next marriage; the introduction of a new word, song or dance explaining a contemporary story, just like a newsreel warning the community of the arrival of disease or climate change; the singing of certain songs appropriate to the young man who has just come from initiation and will publicly dance for the first time with the authority of his new status; the trade of ochres for ceremonial dance body markings. Many ceremonies are layered and coexist at the same time, a living, intersecting web.

In 2024, a year after the failed referendum on the Voice to Parliament, Prime Minister Anthony Albanese attended the Garma Festival in north-east Arnhem Land, where a year earlier he had promised he would hold the vote that previous prime ministers had shied away from. There was hurt and pain and many of the speeches reflected a need to stay strong and powerful in the face of this defeat. A ceremony was enacted where the Prime Minister stood steadfast as groups of dancers with spears threatened him with attack. With frightening closeness, they lunged at him and called out, attempting to make him flinch and show fear. It was indeed concerning as I observed the PM's security detail look agitated and worried, but not the Prime Minister. He stood strong and still, and at the end of the dance he was deemed worthy of receiving a Ganiny or sacred digging stick. It symbolises the restoring of the fire, but to me it looked like the provision of a weapon to continue the fight.

This ceremony was held to acknowledge the fight already fought and the fight that lays ahead for everyone. Among all the talks and speeches, healings and celebrations, this ceremony was the one that was designed for everyone to witness and it demonstrated the strength needed to take on the next fight.

GEORGIA CURRAN

First Nations ceremonies are intrinsically linked to identity and cultural heritage and are often described as being passed down to present-day people from Ancestors who created everything in existence. This understanding of time and history gives these Ancestors as much creative power in the present as they have ever had in the past. It is true not only for First Nations ceremonial leaders but also for many artists more generally, who describe their practices as receiving rather than creating.

In this book we discuss many different types of ceremonies, some having been held continuously since their origins. Others may have laid dormant for periods before being reawakened, and others may have been recently received to negotiate the new contexts that First Nations Australians encounter in a modern world. All are of cultural importance and all honour the long passed-on traditions of generations of forebears.

Across Indigenous Australia, ceremonies often have gendered components. You might hear terms such as 'women's business' or 'men's business', which imply that women's and men's ceremonies are separated from each other entirely and always held in private gender-restricted contexts. It is also common in more public ceremonies involving both men and women for there to be distinct ceremonial roles. In parts of Central and northern Australia, for example, men are often the singers and drive larger-scale ritual events, with women dancing. But these kinds of gendered divisions have often been misrepresented. Not all ceremonies are split along gender lines. While there are certainly strict laws to adhere to, in reality these gendered divides are more blurred and often are shaped by in-the-moment negotiation, inter-gender sharing and particular family and community relations. All ceremony is, in its very nature, an iterative and negotiable act that takes into account context, individual relationships, current politics and numerous other contingencies, including the gendered but complementary roles of men and women.

Many of the anthropologists who practised in Australia in the earlier half of the 20th century were predominantly male. They prioritised working with senior Aboriginal men, who were seen as holding important understandings of non-secular aspects of Aboriginal high-culture. This strongly reflected the Westernised gender prejudices of the period. Senior women were not able to tell a male their business. However Phyllis Kaberry, one of the few female ethnographers from that time, called this out in her book *Aboriginal Woman Sacred and Profane*, published in 1939, but it took the academic world another forty years to really take this seriously and for representations of Aboriginal women to change.[2] In the rise of second-wave feminism throughout the 1970s and 80s, significant ethnographic work focused on the powerful ritual roles of Aboriginal women, though also framed in the biases of Western feminist thinking. Goenpul (Koenpul) woman Aileen Moreton-Robinson pointed this out in her groundbreaking book *Talkin' Up to the White*

Woman, published in 2000. Despite these skewed representations, women across First Nations Australia have continued to manage important ceremonial leadership roles. This is evidenced by the prominence of senior Aboriginal women who drive and oversee community affairs in Australia today.

CEREMONIES TIE TOGETHER THE PAST AND THE PRESENT

Indigenous ceremonies tie present-day people to those of the past in a continuum of passed-on stories, places and memories. But ceremonies are not stagnant and unchanging through time, they are dynamic responses to contemporary contexts. At the 2023 Sydney Festival, Yugambeh dancers performed the long-established Dreamtime story 'How the Birds got their Colours' through a modern fusion of First Nations dance, storytelling and circus. Likewise, ceremonies held in remote areas of Australia that are often considered 'traditional' forms of ancient practices are also entirely contemporary in responding and adapting to contemporary social contexts.

The Kurdiji ceremonies held by Warlpiri people to initiate their young men are conducted with as much vibrancy today as in earlier times, and involve Songlines passed on through generations and linked to Warlpiri Country and ancestral stories for pertinent and current social purposes. No ceremony will ever be exactly the same in form and content as it was in earlier times, and this is vital to its effectiveness through the years and changing circumstances. Songlines and ancestral creation stories are always held in their true form in

Country and can be accessed through time and shifting contexts. In the book *Songlines* in the First Knowledges series, the authors refer to 'broken songlines', which may be disrupted at historical points but in their essence lie as part of a greater whole in Country.[3]

To use an analogy drawn on by Stan Grant in his famous speech 'A World Divided', where he reflects on ideas of identity using an ancient Greek conundrum:

> The ship of the great mythological hero Theseus is kept in dock. Over the years each of its planks is replaced until it is composed entirely of new planks. So here's the question: Is it the same ship? What if each of the old planks was then reassembled to form a new ship – is this then the true ship of Theseus? It's a thought experiment that captures the dilemma of identity. Who are we? Are we the same person today as yesterday? Is our identity fixed or should it reflect the inevitable changes that we all experience over a lifetime.[4]

When we use the word 'traditional' in this book, it is intended to refer to something intrinsically important to peoples' culture and ways of life, something that carries forward stories and values, not in a repeated, stagnant form but in creatively responsive ways to present-day contexts. As peoples' ways of life are continually adapting to their current circumstances, traditions also change and represent these new contexts while maintaining links to practices and ideologies through generations. Wesley discusses the adaptation and evolution of ceremony more in Chapter 5.

TYPES OF CEREMONIES

First Nations ceremonies take various forms and are held for different reasons, but common to all is that they are socially effective in producing change in the world. For Wesley's family, the return of his father to Country, the acceptance of this by his grieving relatives and the formal shifting of the long-established patterns surrounding his life, were all facilitated by the ceremony described in Chapter 1. Likewise, for senior Warlpiri women, the productive power of their yawulyu ceremonies, which I took part in on my first night staying in Yuendumu and for the many years since, allowed the life-force/spirit of an esteemed ceremonial leader to again rest within Country while opening up the related ceremonial songs to continue to be sung and nurture this same life-force/spirit.

In this book we present many examples of ceremonies as they are held in particular social and political contexts today. I give a broad-brush overview here of some types of ceremonies held across First Nations Australia. They encompass huge public spectacles through to personal healing ceremonies, formal initiations through to informal gatherings to share stories, to sing and to dance. Many though not all of the ceremonies described in this book involve musical song and dance, and it is certainly true that in precolonial Australia many ceremonial contexts were centred on song and dance. The types of ceremonies we outline are by no means inclusive because all ceremonies are negotiated in context-specific moments and shift in their form and practice as do the worlds around them.

CORROBOREES

The commonly used word 'corroboree', often associated with First Nations song and dance, appears to have come from south-eastern Australia. This word was quickly appropriated across Australia early in settlement history to describe a ceremony of singing, telling stories and dancing. It has since entered a pan-Aboriginal vocabulary to refer to First Nations gatherings, meetings, celebrations and intergroup encounters of many sorts. As was the case with the corroborees held to manage the encounters First Nations people living in the Sydney region had with the arrival of the British in the years following 1788, these types of ceremonies are a common mode of intergroup engagement across Australia.

The Warlpiri purlapa ceremonies sung by men and women with male dancers is another example of a corroboree-kind of ceremony. My Warlpiri 'cousin', Yamurna Napurrurla Oldfield, recounts going down to the south camp area of Yuendumu most evenings as a child in the 1980s to be part of purlapa ceremonies. She says how everyone – kids, men and women – participated, mostly to have fun. It was a form of entertainment in an era when people did not often travel away from Yuendumu or have other entertainment such as television. Yamurna explains that the main reason they held the purlapa ceremonies was to have a good time! Jerry Jangala Patrick, a senior Elder from the northern Warlpiri community Lajamanu, describes these kinds of community-based public ceremonies as having a clear purpose: 'to make people happy'. The Gurindji song–dance genre wajarra, featured in the book *Songs from the Stations*, with

'Corroboree', pen and ink drawing by Tommy McRae, circa 1986. He was probably a Kwatkwat man, born around 1830.

songs sung by Ronnie Wavehill Wirrpnga, Topsy Dodd Ngarnjal and Dandy Danbayarri at Kalkaringi, similarly indicates a vibrant ceremonial life fostering connectedness and positive feelings amidst the hardships of the station life at Wave Hill.[5]

While the word 'corroboree' has come to describe the more light-hearted, fun activity of celebrations and parties of various sorts, these ceremonial contexts can also have a sacred and serious element. Often at their heart is a story embedded in Country, or a moment of historical importance, or a new encounter with visitors as was thought was the case with the arrival of the First Fleet at what is now called Sydney Cove. Events such as the Deadly Awards and the National Indigenous

Music Awards are also examples of this kind of ceremony. Held each year, these awards recognise and celebrate First Nations' achievements and bring people together in a shared space in a way that develops pride in cultural identity and cohesiveness of community.

RITES OF PASSAGE

French ethnographer and folklorist Arnold van Gennep theorised the idea of 'rites of passage', arguing for their importance in all human social worlds as they are essential to achieving changes in social status and roles throughout people's lives, such as from boy to man, or unmarried to married.[6] He identified three stages of a rite of passage: separation, transition or margin, and incorporation. Obvious examples are funeral ceremonies. There is a moment of separation when a person becomes bereaved, a transitional stage of grieving, and the eventual incorporation of the memory of the deceased person into deep genealogies. In a First Nations context, it is this last stage when the funeral ceremonies are finished that a person's spirit returns to Country and again becomes part of the ancestral life force. Initiatory ceremonies are other examples. The Warlpiri Kurdiji ceremonies, which I discuss further in Chapter 4, centre on young boys leaving their childhood with their mothers and other women (separation), going through ceremony (transition), and then beginning to socialise mostly with other adult men (incorporation). Many communities across Central Australia have a thematically focused version of this Songline, which is central to this ceremony. It involves a group of ancestral women who journey from west to east while being seductively pursued by a male Ancestor of wrong marriage partnership for them. The Seven Sisters Songline featured in the first volume of this series and the exhibition *Songlines: Tracking the Seven Sisters* is another example. As I have described in my book *Sustaining Indigenous Songs*, the Karntakarnta (group of women) songs sung by Warlpiri men and for which women dance, are central to the main ceremonies through which boys transition into young men in Yuendumu and other Warlpiri communities.[7]

Other common rites of passage centre on shifts to different life stages, including around the birth of babies, the shift to motherhood or fatherhood, and in older age into widowhood.

In the last decade or so, there have been many examples of the return and repatriation of ancestral remains stolen from First Nations and taken to museums in Australia or overseas. Often the return of these Ancestors involves rite of passage-style ceremonies. In 2023, a Warlpiri Ancestor was returned to his Country at Pikilyi, to the north-west of Yuendumu. His remains had been taken from a tree-platform burial when the Mount Doreen cattle station was being established in the 1930s and sent to a museum in Adelaide. Ninety years later, when his descendants brought his remains back, they held ceremonies, including men's purlapa and women's yawulyu ceremonial singing and dancing, as a rite of passage to transition his spirit back to Country.

REVELATORY OR REAFFIRMING CEREMONIES

Many ceremonies are held to consolidate people's retention and transmission of knowledge. This is vital to ensure the strength and continuation of tradition. Many involve complex and detailed knowledge and associated rituals, so it is important that there are opportunities for this reinforcement of memory. This often happens while on Country, but for First Nations people who have been denied the opportunity to access their Country and ceremonial knowledge due to effects of colonisation, revelatory ceremonies can be particularly important ways in which people experience, come to know and hold their cultural heritage strong. Ngarigu linguist Jakelin Troy and colleagues at the University of Sydney revitalised women's songs from the Australian Alps after finding old sheet music documenting a song performed by women of the 'Menero tribe' in 1834.[8] In 2019, they performed this song for the first time in almost two centuries, the main aim being to renew its performative power and consolidate its performance in Country. This performance was followed by the dumping of the biggest snowfall in over 100 years! While these ceremonies are held to reaffirm and ensure that knowledge of how to perform them is maintained by people with these responsibilities, they also keep alive other powerful functions.

In Warlpiri Country, women hold twice-yearly dance camps at outstations in their Country, where they sing and dance their yawulyu songs over a four-day long weekend. The main purpose for holding these camps is to allow older women to sing together, reinforcing their memories of the Songlines and Country so that they are maintained

Warlpiri women painting up with Mala kuruwarri 'Rufous Hare Wallaby Dreaming designs' from Jila (Chilla Well).
Pictured: Nancy Nungarrayi Collins (being painted), (left–right) Maisie Napurrurla Wayne, Peggy Nampijinpa Brown, Alice Nampijinpa Michaels and Marlette Napurrurla Ross.

for the future. They also provide a space for younger generations of Warlpiri women to participate in yawulyu and take part in the dancing associated with their Country and grow strong connections to this part of their cultural heritage. These dance camps often involve ceremonies with clear functions, such as smaller healing ceremonies and conflict-resolution dances, and the senior women delight in teasing each other by singing songs to attract lovers! The main focus, however, is on teaching younger women and girls about their connections to their Country and Dreamings, so they can be strong with this knowledge and have active participations in ceremonies.

CEREMONIES OF EXCHANGE AND TRADE

Many very elderly First Nations people living in Central and northern Australia remember an era when, as children, they travelled with their families to visit neighbouring groups for the trade and exchange of ceremony. Often these were centered on gatherings for ceremonies for boys to become young men. The trips involved long distances and the trade of material goods such as ochre, shell and ritual objects, as well as ceremonial songs, dances and designs. These gatherings were crucial in setting up interregional alliances and brought groups together in strong relational ways through facilitating intermarriage.

The Kimberley Aboriginal Law and Culture Centre (KALACC) has in recent years been driving projects to revive these trade routes.[9] Describing this project, Ngarrindjeri Elder Moogy Sumner says, 'We're trading knowledge for dances and we're trading dances for knowledge, we're doing this and it's all about trading ceremony.' Kungarakany and Arrernte man Shaun Angeles, who has also been involved in these projects and works through the Strehlow Research Centre on remote Indigenous collections, explains the main aim is to 're-establish these relationships that our Old People had with different tribes and language groups'.

These stories from the past, oral histories of today's Elders and ethnographic documentation suggest that more than any requirement to hunt or gather for food or water sources, ceremonial activities were the main reason why people travelled around this region so expansively and were crucial to keeping Indigenous economies strong across vast areas. As testament to the long distances involved, a recent study has shown a song called 'Wanji-wanji' was traded across several thousands of kilometres, from Esperance on the south coast of Australia to Port Augusta, throughout Central Australia to the Pilbara, as far north as Broome, and as far east as Wilcannia.[10]

DIPLOMACY CEREMONIES

Diplomacy ceremonies involve a series of exchanges of ceremonial materials and objects of importance between different groups and are recognition of other groups' roles in an established relationship of reciprocity.

The Welcome to Country that opens most major events in Australia today is an example of diplomacy ceremonies focused on forming relational bonds between previously unconnected groups. This type of ceremony honours the deep traditions established through trade and exchange, in which entry on to another Aboriginal group's Country must be welcomed by the Traditional Owners. In Chapter 3, Wesley outlines these ceremonies in detail and the protocols around how they should be held.

Across the Top End of Australia, ceremonies known as Rom are further examples of those with diplomatic purposes. Ethnomusicologist Stephen Wild explains that 'Rom belongs to a genre of ritual in Arnhem Land whose purpose is to promote friendship between people who normally live apart, speak different languages and follow different customs.'[11] A Rom was held in Canberra in 1982 by an Anbarra group from north-central

Arnhem Land to recognise the role that the Australian Institute for Aboriginal Studies (AIAS, now AIATSIS) had in maintaining records of Anbarra culture. Wild writes: 'The empathy achieved by the performers with their audience was a measure of the potential for cross-cultural communication through the performing arts between Aboriginal and other Australians.' A time capsule was then presented to the Anbarra group to open five years later.

A modern example of this kind of diplomacy ceremony was at the Garma Festival in 2023, when the Gumatj dancers were joined by Abdi Karya, a man from Sulawesi in Indonesia. Despite this being Karya's first time in Yolŋu Country, the shared buŋgul dance honoured relationships going back centuries between Aboriginal people from Arnhem Land and traders from Makassar who travelled there by pinisi boats for the trade of fish and sea cucumbers.[12]

Many Aboriginal groups across Australia have long had ceremonies that assist in the resolution of conflict. Makarrata, a peace-making ceremony held in Arnhem Land, is now widely known since it featured in the film *Ten Canoes* and is written about in the Uluṟu Statement from the Heart. In recent years, it has been drawn on in a national political space as a method to encourage more effective reconciliation between Indigenous and non-Indigenous Australians. In *Ten Canoes*, a dispute arises following an accidental killing. Makarrata is then held in which two men from the central group from the Arafura swamp region must face up to having spears thrown at them by the other group. Once the makarrata has taken place these groups agree to move forward without further bad feelings.[13] The book *Law* in this series details the makarrata in *Ten Canoes* and its effectiveness in resolving disputes.[14]

In Central Australia, grand ceremonies known as Jardiwanpa and Ngajakula have been held to resolve conflict between family groups, and they involved the ritualised assault of one group on another with burning branches. While these ceremonies may appear to be pure vendetta, the actions are balanced by particular people who have ceremonial roles that ensure no one is hurt too badly. Without these people the role of the ceremonies in conflict resolution would be ineffective and likely cause further feuds.

SMALLER PERSONAL CEREMONIES

Aside from the grand spectacles and festivals, there are many smaller and very personal First Nations ceremonies. Sometimes they may involve only a few people or a particular family and are highly functional. Examples include healing ceremonies, ceremonies that nurture Country and the growth of plants and animals, those that set up romantic relationships between individuals, and in some cases those in which sorcery is performed to ensure that misfortune befalls an enemy. At these ceremonies, songs are sung in small groups or even by an individual to retain a degree of privacy due to their personal nature.

Some ceremonial events may have a specific objective. For Warlpiri women, the singing of particular yawulyu as nyurnu-kurlangu ('healing songs') has significant power. When I lived in Yuendumu in the mid-2000s and spent most of my days with elderly female ceremonial leaders and singers, it was common for there to be constant pressure on good singers to assist with ailments, whether they were arthritic knees or stomach ulcers. At a recent women's ceremonial camp-out involving large numbers of women, my friend Janet Napurrurla Gordon was having immense difficulty with her sore knees; they prevented her from dancing and moving around easily. Prior to the ceremonial dancing to be held one evening, a group of five senior women took Janet to a private space where she lay down. The women proceeded to sing the Jardiwanpa (Inland Taipan snake) yawulyu, after she had already been painted with the designs on her chest. I was told to move away from Janet's feet as the snake was going to come out that way. As the women sang, they massaged Janet's legs with oil and red ochre. That night Janet got up with all the other Napurrurla and Nakamarra women and danced Jardiwanpa yawulyu to the delights of the crowd who had assumed she would be unable to move. These ceremonies infused the healing life forces of Country within people's bodies and spirits. Yawulyu are frequently used for these kinds of productive purposes – not only do they heal individuals from illness, but they can attract lovers (yilpinji) or assist in resolving disharmony between people.

These kinds of ceremonies are centred on clear and context-specific purposes, be they to unite different groups, assist with social harmony or to promote the health of Country. Most of the ceremonies described in this chapter can have many purposes and may cross between these definitions in their function depending on changing social contexts.

3

WELCOMES, SMOKING AND RITES OF PASSAGE

WESLEY ENOCH

The Welcome to Country has become one of the ceremonies most commonly witnessed in recent years. From the opening of parliaments, public events or even the landing of a plane, we can expect the ceremony of being welcomed to Country or acknowledging Country, depending on the protocols governing this practice, to be part of the proceedings. There is a clear distinction between the two and often people confuse a Welcome to Country with an Acknowledgement of Country, or conflate them as being the same.

A Welcome to Country is given by a Traditional Owner of the Country on which you are gathering. They have the cultural authority, the custodianship to that Country, the connections to those who hold the stories of that place and who can speak of the traditions, history and people who have lived there for thousands of generations, in most cases. It is like when you go to someone's house and knock on the door, only those who live in that house can welcome you in and explain the rules by which the household operates – 'Please take off your shoes.' 'Keep the noise down, Grandma is sleeping.' 'It's safer if we move to the back of the house.'

It would be unusual if as a visitor, you were to open the door and walk into someone's home without being welcomed. In many ways it would be insulting to assume you could just barge in. It could also be dangerous if you came in without being aware of how the home works. Those who live there have a very detailed understanding of the plants and animals, spirits, weather patterns, dangers and opportunities that are found in and around it. Think of the land around you not as something empty and without ownership, rather, all the land in Australia has Traditional Owners and Custodians.

Sometimes we use those terms, Traditional Owner or Custodian, when we are discussing those people who have family links to the land on which they are living. Not all First Nations people are living on the Country they are related to, though. For many, the government policies of forced removals and Stolen Generations, coupled with the search for economic, educational or medical benefits means there has been much movement of our peoples across the continent and the world, so living off Country is a reality for these people. I grew up on the mainland and have lived in several cities around the nation but now I live on the traditional lands and waters of my forebears.

Though I would be entitled to do Welcomes to Country, I choose not to in deference to seniority and respect for those who have lived on Country longer than me. It is always best to talk to senior people about a Welcome to Country rather than placing the burden on younger Traditional Owners.

A Welcome to Country is a ceremony that has been enacted for millennia. Before roads and trainlines and the other ways of travel, First Nations people would cross vast tracts of the continent regularly for hunting, trade and exchange, ceremony and family connection. Sometimes this may have meant travelling over Country to reassert a song or creation story, or it could have been a seasonal journey in search of food or to obtain special ceremonial ochres. As told to me by Elders, before travelling to another place as a visitor you would make camp outside the borders of the Country you wish to go to, signal your intentions and wait for an invitation to enter. This could take hours, days or even weeks. The sign might be campfire smoke, despatching a message stick or a verbal message to others you came across on your travels. The Traditional Owners would receive this message and would meet you along a natural border of the Country – maybe a river, range of hills, a waterhole – where there they would ascertain the merit of your intentions and welcome you or not. This welcome could take many forms, depending in part on whether you were meeting old friends, relatives, trading partners or strangers. There could be an exchange or joint singing of songs, maybe trade, news including updates around cultural burning or weather patterns, but primarily a welcome would include a strong call out to the spirits and Ancestors to give the visitors safe passage through the land. Without this spiritual coverage it is believed the visitor could be susceptible to bad spirits, illness and accidents.

WHAT MAKES A GOOD WELCOME TO COUNTRY?

There is no clear answer here. I have received so many beautiful Welcomes as I've travelled across the landscape. Aunty Joy Murphy and Aunty Di Kerr are both Wurundjeri Elders from the Melbourne area, and in their Welcomes they talk about the borders of their Country and give everyone a leaf from a gum tree, symbolising the respect needed from the deepest root to the tips of the highest branches. They talk about showing respect to Bungul, the Creator Spirit, and the children of Bungul as an important obligation for each visitor.

In the Brisbane area I have seen singing and dancing alongside the sharing of information about family and clan and traditional ownership. There is a strong emphasis on educating visitors about the Traditional Owners, their history, traditions and sovereignty. There is a song called 'Gari Gynda Narmi' (there are multiple spellings for this song) that is often sung and danced during a Welcome to Country throughout the region, and it is also accepted as a farewell song.

In the Sydney area I have been Welcomed many times by Uncle Allen Madden, who is a great entertainer. In his Welcomes he tells jokes and makes you laugh, but he also talks of the borders of the Eora peoples and the twenty-nine clans that make up the Eora Nation. Some of the jokes are proper 'Dad jokes' that are repeated each time. I recently asked Uncle Allen why the jokes were important and why he would tell the same ones at each Welcome, and he said that only through repetition do people learn; the jokes are designed to relax you and make you more receptive to the information he is sharing. By hearing the same information over and over people begin to understand the enormity of the responsibility of coming onto Country. I listened to Uncle Allen's Welcome again recently with all its familiar cadence and inflections, the Dad jokes and information, and for the first time after hearing it perhaps hundreds of times, I heard it more like a song being sung. I recognised patterns I could remember and repeat, like an old song with powerful rhythm and structure, with familiar words of engagement and knowledge. This time, instead of laughing I watched the crowd respond and engage as Uncle Allen intended; they listened to him, heard him, and I thought, Clever old bugger.

ACKNOWLEDGEMENT OF COUNTRY

An Acknowledgement of Country is given when you are not from that place but wish to acknowledge the groups who are. Usually, a senior person acknowledges the Country you are visiting, living or working on. This may come in response to a Welcome to Country by a member of the local custodian group, which is sometimes referred to as the host community. Acknowledgements are about keeping alive the respect for the local people and reinforcing their authority and custodianship. Using again the example of a house, an Acknowledgment is the equivalent of saying 'That's where you live, that's where your family come from.' For those who have already been told, it reminds them that if they ever want to go inside, they know who to talk to and who to be respectful of.

There are many ways to do Welcomes and Acknowledgements, and each group will do them their own way. Here are some of the common elements I have witnessed.

A Welcome often recognises Elders and other First Nations people in the gathering, passes on important information about the Country you are visiting – which could be about its history and traditional knowledges including language, song, dance – introduces the names of the people of the land and their borders, engages you in an exchange and informs you of your obligation to the land, and asks the spirits to look after you as you travel through the Country.

An Acknowledgement of Country often includes a recognition of the Traditional Owners of the land on which you are visiting, names them and pays respect to the Elders of that Country. You can also acknowledge the person or people who performed a Welcome for you some time before and add a piece of information you have learnt about the Country you are on.

SMOKING CEREMONY

The other ceremony you commonly see today is a smoking ceremony. Smoke from a small fire, which is carried or is burning on the ground, is used to ward off bad things and bad spirits and to cleanse people and spaces before they take part in an activity together. This could be before a meeting, family gathering or another important occasion, or it could be for a new building or a space in which an activity is to occur.

Many cultures use smoke to cleanse a space. In North America (Turtle Island) there is a practice called smudging where a person might use a bundle of sage leaves, tobacco, sweet grass or cedar to cleanse or smudge a place of negative energies. In the Catholic Church incense laced with frankincense and myrrh is used in a swinging censer to purify the congregation and symbolise the prayers wafting upward to heaven. Frankincense oil is said to have healing properties, with the power to kill some bacteria and fungi. In Australia smoke has been used for generations as a way of cleansing and preparing the way.

The practice usually involves creating slow burning coals and embers and then adding green leaves to create smoke. Different leaves are used around the country. The most common are those from gum trees, which create a thick acrid, eucalyptus smoke; the oils from the leaves are carried through the smoke and cover hair, clothes and skin. If you have had the chance to stand near a smoking campfire, you will know how you can smell the smoke on your hair and clothes for days. People in other parts of the country may do a mix of leaves, including acacia, bottlebrush and tea-tree, to temper the smell of the gum leaves. In Western Australia there is a practice of using the gum of the grasstree or the Balga to create smoke. This smoke when ingested is said to be good for clearing airways and sinuses. It is no accident that the smoke of these different plants has its own medicinal properties, and the cleansing is both spiritual and a physical healing. I once went to a smoking in New South Wales where the Elder added a range of moss and fungi to the mix of different leaves. The smoke that came from it had a sweet smell and fully prepared us for the meeting ahead.

I have seen smokings occur in several ways. The most common is to use a receptacle such as a coolamon or a metal bucket to hold the hot coals and then to place the smoking leaves or other materials on top. The receptacle can be carried around a gathering to smoke the people and the place. Another way is to build a campfire and add the leaves and other plants over the coals. Then people come to the smoke, walking to it, through it and bathing in it.

There is no 'right' way to be the receiver of the smoke except to think of it as washing your whole body and not leaving any part unsmoked. Imagine washing yourself in the smoke – splashing it on your face and hair, under your armpits, up and down your arms, scooping it up and behind you to fall down your back, splashing it up on to your chest, pulling it into you, wafting the smoke around your body, and lifting your feet to smoke the soles, behind your legs and calves. I was always taught not to turn your back on someone offering you the smoke if they are carrying it around, but I think it is different when the smoke comes from a campfire. I suppose it is only good manners to face the person who is offering you something so important.

The practice of using smoke and fire as a cleanser and for clearing the air is ages old. On this continent fire was also used as a farming tool to clear the land and encourage the movement of fauna from area to area. Kangaroos and other herbivores returned to a place that had been burnt to eat the sweet new shoots of grasses and bushes. In modern times fire has become something to be feared, but before contact it was seen as an important tool that was connected with food, storytelling, farming, communications, and much more. Fire could be made through friction; by rubbing a hard wood into a soft wood, you could create enough friction and heat to ignite small shavings from the soft wood. There were many ways to carry fire from campsite to campsite; for example, by using a spent banksia seed pod that could burn as a low coal for a very long time.

An Elder talked to me about the power of the smoke and the smoking. The smoke helps bring confidence that a place is clear of bad spirits, or it cleanses a person so they can come fresh to an activity. The Elder also talked about the power of smell to unite a group. During and straight after a smoking ceremony, we all smell the same regardless of where we have come from. At events that ran over several days, I was told not to wash my hair or clothes during that time, so the smell might linger for as long as possible and extend the protection it offered.

Smell is an important signifier of power and authority. Sometimes to give a blessing an Elder might wipe their 'smell' on you. By giving you their 'smell', they are lending you the cloak of their authority to travel to another place or to visit people. The Elder might wipe their armpits with their hands and then brush their hands down your shoulders and arms. The strong power of smell is there to protect you from things that might threaten you on your way. There is a story of the early days of the colony in Sydney that tells of some of the local Eora people who, when approaching the British, were covered in emu fat. The smell of the fat was so strong that the potential 'evil spirits' or 'ghosts' could not bring bad things upon the locals; instead, it helped to ward them off and protect the people. The stronger the scent the more power it has. Even today the smell of a person is an important signifier of authority and cultural strength, of health and power. In the Torres Strait, talcum powder and sweet-scented sprays and perfumes are used as a form of appreciation. Sometimes when people are dancing it is not unusual for others to give a sign of their appreciation and encouragement by spraying a dancer with perfumes or deodorants, or by shaking talcum powder on the backs of the best dancers. The smell is a sign of community bonding and building, and the dancer can walk around the gathering with the smell or the visible signs of the talcum powder.

CEREMONIES AND PRACTICES FOR GRIEF

There are several traditions that you might know around television and radio programs that depict or mention Aboriginal and Torres Strait Islander people who have passed away. Here is one from SBS:

> *WARNING: Aboriginal and Torres Strait Islander viewers are warned that the following program may contain images and voices of deceased persons.*

These statements act as a warning to First Nations people, as it is highly irregular to cultural grieving practices to see images, hear the voices or say the name of people recently deceased. In fact in many cultures it is considered distressing and traumatising. I was told that maintaining the presence of the person who is recently deceased doesn't allow them to pass on and ties them to this existence when they must go. I believe it is an important part of the grieving process that the deceased is released and their family and friends are given respite from constant consideration of their loss.

As we have written earlier, in some communities it's normal not to say the name of the deceased even if someone else in that community shares the same name. Imagine someone is named Sally and they pass away, everyone in that community and maybe in related communities could not say the name Sally for a length of time. This means that the name Sally is put away for a time period to mark respect and allow the spirit unimpeded release. If your name is Sally and you are a close relative to the deceased Sally, your name might be put away for a number of years or until an Elder in your family deems it the right time for the name to be used again. If you are a more distant relation or associate, you might find the name is put away for less time. During this period you might be given a 'no name' to replace your name, like the name Kumunjayi in Yuendumu. So instead of being called Sally you would be known as Kumunjayi for the mourning period.

This practice has extended into the digital era where video and audio recordings are put away for a similar length of time, or where the express permission of families must be granted for the general public to receive news of the person. This was the case for the famous Yolŋu award-winning singer and multi-instrumentalist Geoffrey Gurrumul Yunupingu from Elcho Island. After his passing the family members gave permission for him to be referred to as Dr G and for his image to be used so that the media could accurately report his passing. In *The 7 Stages of Grieving*, a play I wrote with Deborah Mailman in 1995, this idea of removing images was discussed; after the death of a family member the image of that person was put away in a small wooden box under the 'stereo in the front room'. This practice can also mean that it is not possible to erect a tombstone until at least a year or so after the person's death; only then can their name and image can be displayed. Sometimes a tombstone can remain shrouded until a moment of revealing. The people of the Torres Strait will hold a Tombstone Opening or Revealing ceremony to reveal the tombstone of a loved one. It is a community event that completes the grieving process and brings closure for the family.

In some communities in the south-east of the continent it was also a practice to layer on a thick clay 'cap' to the head of grieving women to show the clan that these women were in mourning. The weight of the cap would affect their everyday actions and represent the weight of their grief. Eventually, over weeks or months, the cap would break apart as it wore away naturally, which symbolised the release of grief. In some Central Australian communities, the act of inflicting physical pain on yourself by striking the side of your head with your fist or a stone could be used to release the emotional pain of grief. Ultimately, ceremonies and rituals dealing with death and grieving the world over are all about shaping and containing the pain of loss and offering a way to help navigate a future life.

THE CEREMONIES OF MARRIAGE

Though marriage in a modern Western context is between two people, marriages in many First Nations communities are more complicated. It is no accident that one of the first things First Nations people do when they meet you is attempt to work out where you come from and if they are related to you and how. There are ceremonies of identification and exchange that must be entered into to work out where you fit into a network of relationships.

Through a complex system of skin names and moieties, women and men have set relationships and obligations within the clan. Families are differentiated by a web of obligations to Songlines, animals and places, and many aspects of cultural life are built into maternal and paternal genetic lines. You are born into a distinct relationship to the landscape, flora and fauna and inherited responsibilities to care for them and maintain those obligations. The finely balanced relationships are set out in an ever-moving generational map of connections. This birth right comes with obligations to marry only from the skin groups that match the preordained order of the relationship. Think of skin as a necessary organising principle for all the relationships in your life; you have aunts and uncles, parents, siblings, cousins, grandparents and even some people you can never talk to (because they are poison cousins). Now consider a world where everyone in your community is related to you and you have to work out who you can and can't date and marry. This is where skins come in.

A child could be considered like a grandparent to you, your uncles can be your fathers, and even though you don't share the same parents someone could be your sister. This is as complicated as it sounds trying to explain it. Ultimately, there are limitations to the people who are the right match for you through appropriate skin names. You might find these obligations match people of different generations, that is, an older woman and a teenager or an elderly man and a much younger woman. These relationships can be decided from birth due to the skin relationships. This is a system designed to avoid inbreeding and genetic abnormalities in a tight community. The term 'wrong skin' refers to a relationship that does not conform to the cultural law. Marrying 'wrong skin' can be disastrous for the clan and in some instances mean banishment, or worse.

Marriages can indicate relationships of care and responsibility. If you have the capacity to care for and provide for more than one wife or husband, you may be asked to take up a greater responsibility in the clan and marry others so you can maintain cultural business and fulfill expectations within the families.

This is all by way of saying that ceremonies around marriage are complex. They represent an expansive set of relationships that need to be acknowledged in a wedding.

SHIFTING FROM ONE STATE OF BEING TO ANOTHER

As we wrote in Chapter 2, there are many ceremonies that are public and openly invite observation. These celebrations usually take the form of a 'festival', where dancing and singing are a shared experience, where trade and business can be done. Others are secret sacred, held away from the glare of cameras. They might run over many days, with specific song and dance and rituals. Initiation is a rites-of-passage ceremony that may represent a range of factors for different First Nations people – they may include age, cultural knowledge, tests of hunting and skills-based proficiencies, through to scarification, circumcision and the removal of teeth. It can be an intimate ceremony that sets aside the child and ushers in the adult with a test of fortitude and resilience. In the modern era, initiation ceremonies have found their way into competitive sports, educational settings, risk behaviours and social events, such as debutante balls. Moving beyond childhood, the individual can demonstrate their skills and present to the world as an adult.

All ceremony is about the telling of stories and the shift from one state of being to another. Ceremonies restate where we have come from through story, song, dance and repeated intergenerational actions, great moments of community bonding and reassertion of bonds. Ultimately, ceremony is about transferring our cultural knowledge through time, connecting our past with our future.

4

WORLDS OF RELATIONSHIPS – WARLPIRI CEREMONIES HELD TODAY

GEORGIA CURRAN

Ceremonies are and likely always have been important for First Nations groups across Australia as ways to maintain relationships and honour longstanding social networks. Nowadays, First Nations people can use ceremonial performances to connect with others more broadly and represent themselves on a global stage. This chapter focuses on some of the ceremonies held in the remote Central Australian community of Yuendumu, where I have worked with Warlpiri families for the last two decades. These ceremonies have been passed on through generations from the timeless and ongoing creational moment known by Warlpiri people as Jukurrpa.

Ancestral Beings originally created and held these ceremonies, and Jukurrpa stories are pivotal to these ceremonial events. I include some ceremonies that, until recent decades, were central to the socialisation and maturity of many senior Warlpiri people. Although no longer held, these ceremonies deeply influenced these people's approach and leadership in current ceremonial life.

This overview of Warlpiri ceremonial life is certainly not intended to be representative of that of other First Nations groups, though there are some similarities with neighbouring groups in Central Australia as well as further afield. Across Australia, First Nations people have had vastly different experiences and encounters with colonisation, which have had deep impacts on ways in which ceremonial traditions have been passed on to the present day.

WARLPIRI CEREMONIES

I have had the immense privilege and honour of participating in ceremonies with Warlpiri families over many years. When I began working in the Central Desert I was a twenty-three-year-old student. I spent several years travelling around Central Australia with Warlpiri families to attend various ceremonies, as well as participating in those that occurred during the times when I was living in Yuendumu. There are many stories in this book about ceremonies that I have been involved in with Warlpiri families, mostly as this is the avenue through which I have come to understand these matters. As I attend other First Nations ceremonies in other parts of Australia, including Welcome to Countries, larger festivals involving many different groups and stage performances, this background frames the way I participate and understand them.

When I first arrived in Yuendumu, I was greeted by a group of women – Ruth Oldfield, Ena Spencer and Lucy Kennedy – all Napaljarri skin and good friends with my PhD supervisor Mary Laughren, also a Napaljarri. They saw it was appropriate for me to be a Nungarrayi, their niece (brother's daughter) so that I was in a relationship for them to teach me and also given I was Mary's student. In a patrilineal system of inheritance, the aunt–niece (father's sister–brother's daughter) relationship of this sort is the way knowledge of Jukurrpa, Country, songs and ceremonies is taught among women. This skin name determines my participatory roles in Warlpiri ceremonies and the ways in which I do collaborative documentation-style research with Warlpiri families. This background has led to many projects that provide practical support for ceremonial events and empower present generations to use new resources and technology to maintain and revitalise their cultural heritage. Like the learning spirals that Wesley mentioned in Chapter 2, as I have been around with Warlpiri families over the years in Yuendumu, I have found that different levels of knowledge and different ways of appreciating and participating in the same ceremonies have emerged. I am deeply grateful to the juju-ngaliya (senior ritual leaders) for including me in this way.

Today Warlpiri people hold ceremonies for contemporary social purposes but these practices have deep roots in the past, linking to ways of life that have changed significantly in recent decades. As such they are also important records of history and cultural heritage. Warlpiri people once lived dispersed across their Country in small family groups and travelled around largely for inter-family ceremonial events. Since the establishment of cattle stations across the remote desert region in the 1930s, more and more people came to live in centralised settlement areas. Yuendumu is one such settlement, established in 1946 as a government reserve. Some reports from older Warlpiri people and ethnographers such as Françoise Dussart note that moving to the settlements in some ways increased the intensity of ceremonial activity as it meant people no longer had the logistical challenges of getting together, and increased the necessity to keep social harmony between families.

In communities such as Yuendumu, large-scale ceremonies connect family groups and maintain social networks across Warlpiri Country, as well as more broadly with other Aboriginal groups across the Central and Western Deserts and beyond. Holding these ceremonies is important as they help to maintain social order and systems, which have sustained populations in this region for millennia. As mentioned earlier, it is common across Central Australia to talk about ceremonies as 'business' – a particularly appropriate term given that for many senior Warlpiri people upholding ceremonial obligations is their main occupation. It involves serious work, time commitment, negotiation and facilitation skills, as well as high levels of expertise in detailed religious knowledge and attention to its proper practice. The word 'religion' is used here and throughout this book with reference to the structured spiritual practices that underpin Warlpiri worldviews and beliefs. Ceremonies are owned and organised by particular people – Warlpiri kirda (owner) rights are inherited from your father and kurdungurlu (management responsibilities) are inherited from your mother and her father. I have to emphasise here, as it is reiterated to me by senior Warlpiri people, that these ceremonies are productive; they are held with purpose and to achieve particular outcomes.

The ceremonies I write about in this chapter are some of the main public ceremonies held in Yuendumu today. There are other private and sometimes restricted ceremonies held in gendered male and female groups, as outlined in Chapter 2, but the community-focused ceremonies discussed here are broadly shared. They illustrate the importance of these long passed-on ceremonies in the day-to-day lives of people in this region of Central Australia.

KURDIJI – CEREMONIES FOR MAKING YOUNG MEN

When I first came to live in Yuendumu, just prior to the summer of 2005–2006, I soon found myself travelling with Warlpiri families to a nearby community known as Wariyiwariyi (also Mount Allan or Yuelamu). A large ceremony ground had been cleared to the east of the community area and many local families as well as other groups like ours that had travelled from their communities had set up camp nearby. Several bough shelters were erected for shade close to the cleared area to guard against the intense Central Australian heat. Our group camped in this area for the next month or so.

My good friend from Yuendumu, who was married to a man from Wariyiwariyi, had recently had a baby and her in-laws often visited our camp. Her father-in-law, Jack Jangala Cook, was one of the senior ceremonial leaders in Wariyiwariyi and each time he came to visit us he would tell us which teenage boys had 'been caught' (meaning they'd been noticed by senior men as being of the right maturity to go through these ceremonies and escorted to a secluded bush site for preparation), and he would let us know when the ceremonies were to occur. Across about a five-week period there were three all-night ceremonies, each followed by a shorter afternoon ceremony the next day. In between, men and women would do separate activities surrounding these events and in preparation for these grand all-night events. With groups of women, I would often spend days gathering ochres, or sometimes 'locked down' in our camp while the men were travelling – a precautionary measure taken to ensure that we did not accidentally encounter the men's activities that are part of the restricted aspects of the ceremonies.

During my first summer participating in Kurdiji, Jangala was living near to where we were camping with his two wives and their children, and one of his teenage sons would be 'going through' in an upcoming ceremony. As my skin name was Nungarrayi, Jangala often joked that he might make me his third wife. Despite this clearly being in fun, my ceremonial role as 'mother' to his son was a more serious obligation. During one all-night ceremony, I danced in a line with the other 'mothers' and a burning firestick was passed among us during the evening. I held it in front of me while I danced as the other mothers had done, occasionally taking it back to the fire to ensure it would keep burning. Over the following days and months, I was told that I'd really danced well and done my proper job. I learned that dancing with a firestick in this way also was a way of setting up a 'promised marriage'. While I had no children of my own at this point, it became evident that this act meant that my yet-to-be-conceived future daughter would be 'promised' to one of the young men going through the ceremony! Several months later, Jangala arrived at an outstation where I was camped with families from Yuendumu and produced from his car a beautiful painting of the Watiyawarnu (Acacia seed) Jukurrpa, his own Country, and presented it to me, noting that he was 'just squaring things up' between us. This was a friendly gesture in which my efforts at his son's Kurdiji ceremony were acknowledged without the obligations they required.

Kurdiji, as it is known in Warlpiri, is more broadly referred to as 'young men's business' across Central Australia. These ceremonies are held every summer in many Central Australian communities and are a main preoccupation for most people in the period immediately following Christmas and up until late February when the school year resumes. This time of year is marked by its intense heat; many community organisations shut down for summer and the predominantly whitefella employees from the organisations go back to their homes on the east coast of Australia. Across the region, a different kind of structure emerges. The long hot days are often spent resting, with most activity beginning as the sun nears the western horizon and it cools down. Ceremonial activities are prominent during this time and Warlpiri mobs sing their Songlines in the ceremonial contexts that are key to their present-day lives.

During an interview I conducted with esteemed Warlpiri Elder, the late Harry Jakamarra Nelson, in 2018 (only a few years before he passed away) he emphasised that:

> We sing all our songs, the Jukurrpa, at Kurdiji mainly today, which is young men's business but also where the women dance. That's where all our laws come from – it is a big Jukurrpa that bring all the people together. Kurdiji is not just for making young men, it's the Jukurrpa – it's everyone's Jukurrpa.

Jakamarra had been a leader for Kurdiji and ceremonial life in Yuendumu for a large part of his life and left a gaping hole for succession to this role, though many middle-aged men are now stepping up. At the Kurdiji ceremonies held over the summer of 2023–2024, thirty-eight young men were 'put through business' in one evening – a record in the expansion of this ceremony, which has been dramatically growing with a rising youth population. As recently as the 1980s, only three to four young men would 'go through business' at once. This illustrates the rise in importance of this ceremony, especially since the decline of the Kajirri ceremonies that were central to ceremonial life across the region in the 1980s and which will be discussed more in Chapter 7.

'Kurdiji' is the general word for a shield used to block a hit from a spear or boomerang. It also refers to the first phase of initiation ceremonies. The shields are painted with designs as a central part of the Kurdiji ceremonies as well. This word also refers to the Songlines that are sung in the all-night public ceremony called

Marnakurrawarnu. Different Songlines, relating to different Country and family groups, are sung in the various settlements across Central Australia but the ceremonies are very similar in the way they are held.

The public Marnakurrawarnu ceremony starts early in the morning and continues through to the afternoon with yawulyu (women's ceremonies) and parnpa (men's ceremonies) held in their respective women's and men's groups on opposite sides of a ceremonial ground. These ceremonies are associated with Jukurrpa affiliated with the soon-to-be young men. After this, the all-night part of the Marnakurrawarnu ceremony begins, in which a Songline is sung by men while women dance. This continues until sunrise the next day. Men sit in a group on the eastern part of the ceremonial ground singing and playing boomerang clapsticks, that is, two boomerangs clapped together for rhythm. Women gather in a group just on their western side with their bedding, and throughout the night they get up to dance in a long line from north to south, with a repetitive jumping dance style, their hands slumped to their sides. The women give high-pitched calls at the end of each iteration of asong verse. Today, holding this all-night ceremony makes Warlpiri people feel strong and optimistic for their future, and many Warlpiri families who live in distant places travel back to remote communities to participate. As the late Warlpiri Elder and singer at Kurdiji, Otto Jungarrayi Sims, explained to me after the ceremonies last summer:

> We sing all night so our Warlpiri future generations can keep their Jukurrpa and carry it on in their hearts and spirits. It will keep them strong, the way our Ancestors were, so they don't lose it.

For Kurdiji ceremonies in Yuendumu, men sing the Karntakarnta Songline while playing boomerang clapsticks, which give a strong continuous beat. The women dance, moving slightly forward with a shuffling, forward-leaning style and again with their arms slumped to their sides.[1] The song consist of many verses of two, sometimes three lines and these are each repeated many times over the course of the night. This Songline follows the journey of a group of ancestral women from near Kunajarrayi (Mount Nicker). They actually start their journey further west at Yapurnu (Lake Mackay), a salt lake on the border of the Northern Territory and Western Australia, and end it at Yuluwurru (Lake Lewis), another salt lake just south of Laramba (Napperby). This is a distance of several hundred kilometres, traversing various terrains and travelling through many important sites. In different settlements, song sets associated with different Songlines are performed but they are also referred to as Kurdiji as they are used for the same ceremony. For example, in the more northern Warlpiri community, Lajamanu, the Songline follows the eastward journey of a group of women from Minamina, a site in the west of Warlpiri Country. In Kurdiji ceremonies I attended in Wariyiwariyi, a community predominantly populated by Anmatyerr speaking people, the Songline begins at the salt lake Yuluwurru, the same place where the Yuendumu one finishes, and continues eastwards, joining these two groups such that they can have ceremonies together based on this shared song material. Most senior Warlpiri men in Yuendumu know the songs sung in Lajamanu, Yuendumu, Wariyiwariyi, Laramba, Papunya, and Mount Liebig, and frequently participate in Kurdiji ceremonies in these communities as well as many others across the Central Desert region.

The day after the all-night Marnakurrawarnu a shorter ceremony named Warawata is held in the afternoon. Some of the verses from the song sets sung during the Marnakurrawarnu ceremony are also sung at Warawata but for only about half an hour. In the past, this final stage took the form of an elaborate ceremony called Kirrirdikirrawarnu, which involved big leafy poles and further all-night singing and dancing.[2] Warlpiri people from Yuendumu still participate in Kirrirdikirrawarnu when they go to other settlements but it is no longer held in Yuendumu. In the last thirty years this has been mostly replaced with the much shorter Warawata, which has been borrowed from Pintupi and Luritja groups from the Country to the south.[3] This may be to ease the onerous pressure on a small group of elderly singers to sit up with no sleep for a second night in a row!

The Warawata ceremony begins late in the afternoon after a long sleepy day spent resting after efforts the night before.[4] People walk or drive over to gather on a cleared ground just outside of the community area. Everyone sits down spatially organised by generation moiety and gender. Women sit on the south of the area in two groups and men on the northern side, also in two groups. Generation moieties divide all people in the world into two halves (different halves than the more commonly understood patrimoieties). In this system, as a woman it means that you sit and dance for this ceremony with other women who are classificatory grandmothers and granddaughters, and the other moiety are women who are mothers and daughters. There are many negotiations done during this time guided by the main leader for the ceremonies involving new family alliances formed during the previous night's ceremony. Following these negotiations there is a short dance involving the same songs.

In one of these ceremonies that I attended in 2023, after this initial gathering and organisation, two of the senior men moved to a ceremony ground nearby and stood at the eastern side of the larger group of men, who sat facing west, and made a small fire on their eastern side. The two men held sticks at each end behind their heads. The women, grouped in their generation moieties on either side of the fire, danced westwards in the same shuffling style to the singing of the men. This dance style indicated the travelling of the Ancestors as it did the night before. Unlike the seriousness of the previous night though, this ceremony was a lot of fun, especially for all the kids. The men sped up their singing and the women had to dance faster and faster. At the end, the generation moiety group of women who danced the fastest and kept going for the longest was declared the 'winner'.

Following this all the boys to be initiated went around to the east side of the group to stand behind where the women had just been dancing. The juka (guardians for the boys going through business) appeared, adorned in red ochre, and stood on the southern side. The young boys threw firesticks all the way over the group, appearing as if they were trying to hit them but clearly intentionally missing. Then the juka ran through the middle of the group, picked up the boys and carried them on their shoulders, running back to the south-west. They then threw them up in the air a few times and the boys ran quickly back to the community area in Yuendumu, laughing delightedly as they did so. The mothers of these boys followed their sons, who were now candidates for the ceremonies in the coming years.

Following this the young men who were currently going through business appeared from the bush to the west and walked in to where the men were still sitting. The mothers of these soon-to-be young men reached out for them dramatically, crying and throwing themselves on the ground. I was told this was the last time they would see their sons for a while as they were going to be based in a secluded bush camp for a few months with senior men to look after them. At this point in the ceremony all the women had to leave quickly, with the men shouting at us to go faster.

Leading up to the holding of a Kurdiji there is often a lengthy journey, known as jilkaja, by one of the boys to be initiated with one or two of his juka (guardian) to other Aboriginal communities to inform them of the upcoming ceremony. The jilkaja may include half a dozen communities, the farthest of which might be many hundreds of kilometres from his home. When the boy reaches the most distant one the party turns around and on the journey back calls in to those communities they have visited already to gather people to travel to the boy's home community to participate in the ceremony. This results in very large parties of people travelling long distances across the desert to end up at ceremony. In picking up people from other communities and escorting them with their families back to their home community, inter-family alliances are formed that are maintained through lifetimes, as well as subsequent generations, in established systems of reciprocity. One account of a jilkaja saw parties of Warlpiri families gathered from Lajamanu and Yuendumu travelling all the way back to the boy's home community of Tjuntjuntjara in Western Australia, 2250 kilometres away, only to stay for a few days and then turn around and drive the same distance back to Lajamanu via Yuendumu.[5] While one young man may be the focus, the efforts that go into these ceremonies and the distances travelled are indicative of the contemporary importance of setting up interregional family alliances.

These kinds of jilkaja journeys and Kurdiji ceremonies establish connections between families and between the young men who go through Kurdiji together (known as age-brothers) that last a lifetime. For women, the days of these jilkaja are spent sleeping during long car trips or waiting in camps for men to finish gender-restricted parts of business; the nights are filled with singing, making food and tea and generally making sure the travelling parties are safe from intruders of all sorts – be they strangers, drunks or lurking kurdaitcha (monstrous threatening beings). The songs that women sing during these all-night periods while men are asleep are only in these private settings, never in public, although they are heard clearly by everyone in the camp.

The contemporary Lajamanu-based justice body, also called Kurdiji, carries forth the same themes of justice and maintenance of law and community harmony, using the same symbolism of 'the shield' as protection, and carrying the shared connotations of community cooperation and commitment to wellbeing of future populations that Warlpiri people understand to be fundamentally what Kurdiji ceremonies are about.

A year or two after a Kurdiji ceremony, a second ceremony used to be held called Kankarlu, which incorporated different genres of song (primarily parnpa, a genre of private men's song). Most elderly men who live in Yuendumu today have been through Kankarlu and describe it as 'high school' but it is perhaps more similar to university – a time of deep education with knowledgeable Elders spent in Country, learning about the spiritual, social and ceremonial laws of Warlpiri people in the wider region. In the past, it wasn't until young men had finished Kankarlu that they were considered to be proper adults, able to have families and adequately guide future generations in the knowledge required to live respectfully. The ritual events surrounding Kankarlu no longer occur in Yuendumu as young men are not able to spend this significant period with their Elders in the bush, instead being required to attend school or work. However, the older generations frequently reminisce about these ceremonies, recounting the songs, designs, dances and stories they learned at that time. They are concerned about the decline in young men's knowledge of Jukurrpa stories, songs, dances and designs in more recent decades, with Kankarlu no longer being practised and with no replacement forum for learning about higher-level Warlpiri religious life and knowledge of places, ancestral stories and ceremonies.

CONFLICT RESOLUTION CEREMONIES

Warlpiri people are famous for their spectacular Jardiwanpa and Ngajakula ceremonies, particularly so since the making of the Blood Brothers film by Ned Lander and Rachel Perkins *Jardiwarnpa: A Warlpiri Fire Ceremony*, released in 1992.[6] They are often called 'fire ceremonies' in anthropological literature, most likely because of the burning of large leafy branches as a climax to the ceremony, yet their associated Jukurrpa is not linked to fire at all. The popularity among Warlpiri people of these ceremonies may have a lot to do with their incorporation of many different family groups from different places – again reinforcing the importance of ceremony for maintaining social networks and building new ones. It is perhaps this focus on so many people coming together that makes it powerful in conflict resolution – it is not really possible to hold a Jardiwanpa unless everyone can get along well enough to do so!

The songs that are sung by men for these ceremonies are all linked to Jukurrpa stories, which involve an initial fight that is resolved through joint performances of ceremonies. Over several months in 2006, when I was living in Yuendumu, preparations were made for a Jardiwanpa ceremony. Each afternoon, the senior men and women as well as various others, gathered on the eastern ceremonial ground. Unfortunately, the logistical demands of trying to get all the people required for this large-scale ceremony together, and several interruptions including the Kurdiji ceremonies that needed to be held in the coming summer, meant that it was not successful and this ceremony was put on hold to be finished later.[7] Since this time, while some older men still sing the songs necessary for Jardiwanpa, it has not been held.

Women also have smaller Jardiwanpa yawulyu ceremonies in the late afternoon prior to the larger-scale events. With senior Warlpiri women, I have assisted to document some of these songs in a book.[8] Ngajakula is a similar conflict resolution ceremony owned by the opposite patrimoiety *and* is also still known by a few older men.[9]

The primary reason for holding these ceremonies is to open up the possibility of remarriage for widows of deceased men associated with one of the focal Ancestral Beings. As traditionally Warlpiri women were a significant fifteen years younger than their husbands, this is an important political and social decision and one in which many women navigate through their choice to participate or not. A large part of one of the all-night ceremonies involves all the widows dancing in lines with burning firesticks; this performative act facilitates their passage to re-marry. As with other larger scale ceremonies such as the Kurdiji described above, men sing while keeping a strong beat with boomerang clapsticks and the women dance. The women's dance style of shuffling forward with feet barely leaving the ground and hands raised beside the shoulders while vocalising repeated high-pitched sounds is iconic of these ceremonies. Many Warlpiri people refer to the ceremonies in day-to-day speech by mimicking this dance style.

Jardiwanpa and Ngajakula generally take about two weeks to complete, culminating in its spectacular final two nights. Before this, there is a long period of waiting for everyone to arrive. During this time, people move their camps so they can sleep near the ceremonial ground and gather each night to rehearse songs and dances. This will go on until everybody necessary for the ceremony has come together. The initial part consists of men singing in the early afternoon from the central Songline associated with that particular ceremony, as the women are dancing with their hands raised besides their shoulders while vocalising, before switching to a knee-quiver dance incorporating a hand movement similar to winnowing seeds in a coolamon. The dance style changes when the men are singing songs associated with the yankirri Jukurrpa (Emu Dreaming).

This continues until all the people needed to perform this ceremony have gathered in one place. On the final night there is an elaborate ceremony that involves the burning of long poles wrapped with eucalyptus leaves. The Warlpiri kirda (owners) of the ceremony stand together in a tight group while certain managers of the ceremony shake the poles over the owners, showering them in sparks in a kind of ritualised assault. The other group of managers, from the same patrimoiety, is responsible for making sure that the owners standing together do not get too burnt by brushing off the showering sparks. When the ceremonies are finished any issues are deemed resolved. In recent decades, Jardiwanpa is the most popular of the two ceremonies, with many Warlpiri people using Jardiwanpa as a general overarching word for these conflict resolution ceremonies that are performed almost identically despite their links to different Jukurrpa and Country.

WOMEN'S YAWULYU CEREMONIES

Both men and women in Warlpiri worlds have Country-focused ceremonies that nurture connections of individuals through their inherited links to particular places and ancestral stories. While these ceremonies are held in private, women's only contexts for the most part, nowadays there are many yawulyu that are adapted for staged performances, whether they are on festival grounds, concert hall stages or other contexts in which a larger public is invited to view as audience.[10] In Chapter 8, I give some examples of these kinds of staged events and discuss some of the ways in which senior Warlpiri women authorise ceremonies to be adapted for large public audiences.

Yawulyu, which I introduced in Chapter 1, were held to open up the restrictions on holding ceremonies and telling stories connected to a dearly loved woman who had passed away a number of years earlier. The word 'yawulyu' refers to the songs, designs and dances that are performed by small groups of women and represent the identity of a Warlpiri woman and follow the Dreaming itineraries of Ancestral Beings across the Country. Women associate themselves with particular yawulyu according to their connections with Country along these Dreaming itineraries. These songs often have a linked story and often evoke particular places and the activities of Ancestors. Yawulyu may be performed in a song series or as individual verses, often in the context of a wider ritual. There are many verses for each Songline known by Warlpiri women that are repeated many times over the course of the ceremony. These iterations of a verse are then repeated a number of times before moving on to the next verse. The rhythmic text of these songs is fixed but set to a flexible descending melodic line such that each time yawulyu are sung it is a unique performance. As mentioned earlier, some yawulyu are labelled as nyurnu-kurlangu ('healing songs') and are powerful in healing particular illnesses. In these situations, animal fat or cooking oil is 'sung' with these yawulyu and then massaged into the body of the sick woman. Some yawulyu are also labelled as being yilpinji, because when sung for a particular person (or item of their clothing) it makes them more sexually attractive. Other yawulyu evoke places, weather conditions, increase food resources or recount Jukurrpa events. Yawulyu are powerful and productive, like other ceremonies.

In the afternoon before Kurdiji ceremonies, yawulyu associated with the Countries of the female relatives of the young men going through Kurdiji are sung by small groups of women who paint their chests with the associated designs and sing connected songs. From the 1990s until 2010s, women from across Central Australia would gather annually to perform yawulyu for each other over a week in a kind of festival-style showcasing. This will be discussed more in Chapter 7. Many community groups used these opportunities and other festival-like gatherings to demonstrate their unique styles of song and dance. Warlpiri women, who tended to be a dominant group at these events, also used this opportunity to do important business such as 'finishing up' for women who had recently passed away by performing their yawulyu with a specialised yellow ochre ceremony associated with mourning. These 'finishing up' ceremonies were held in an intimate space over an all-night period in Yuendumu. These were also incorporated into more widely attended events such as interregional gatherings. The 'finishing up' yawulyu involved all senior women shifting their camp to a ceremony ground where they sang yawulyu each afternoon after sunset for several hours. The final night consisted of an all-night performance of the same yawulyu.

Nowadays Warlpiri women are proactive in setting up contexts for teaching, learning and practicing yawulyu, as women across generations are aware of the importance for Warlpiri cultural identity. The Southern Ngaliya Warlpiri dance camps are held twice a year at various outstations near to Yuendumu, and they are a key opportunity for women to nurture and pass on the important connections between individuals, their families, Country and Jukurrpa stories that are intrinsic to yawulyu.

Warlpiri women also have the ceremonial genre – yilpinji – centred on love and sexual attraction, as mentioned earlier. Yilpinji are different in their performed structure to yawulyu. Many yilpinji are borrowed from neighbouring regions and brought into the Warlpiri women's repertoires because they are believed to be more effective than their own forms. While Country and ancestral stories may be invoked in yilpinji, their primary function is to attract lovers. Yawulyu and yilpinji share some similarities in musical and linguistic features but are clearly distinct in that yilpinji do not have the same structure to their performance, are performed for individuals rather than groups, and have clear narratives with overtly sexual themes rather than the focus that yawulyu have on evoking Country and ancestral stories.

MEN'S ONLY CEREMONIES

Warlpiri men have many ceremonies ranging from those that are highly restricted to particular senior men to those that are open for large public audiences. Parnpa are one genre of men's songs held in ceremonies for Warlpiri men only. They are often labelled 'increase songs' in ethnographic literature, drawing on one of their functions, which is to make bush food and other resources, such as water, more plentiful. Parnpa ceremonies have other functions, such as to cure illnesses or alter weather conditions. However, their primary function is for young men to learn about Warlpiri ancestral stories and the men's rights and responsibilities to Jukurrpa and Country. As such they are held during the afternoon of the first day of the Kurdiji ceremonies. During these ceremonies it is the father who has the responsibility of painting a shield with designs relating to his Country and Jukurrpa through his paternal line. The fathers also show the young men how to do the dances while the senior men sing. Although parnpa are often discussed as being 'secret' or 'restricted' songs in this context and never openly include women or a more general public, there are many instances, including during Kurdiji, where they are performed in full sight of women, though often at quite a distance such that the songs are inaudible.

Purlapa is a genre of men's ceremony associated with specific Country and ancestral stories, and in the 1970s and 1980s were widely held as a form of community entertainment. Purlapa is accompanied by a strong beat such as clapping together two boomerangs or sticks or hitting a bottle on the ground. It is the only genre of Warlpiri song in which men and women sing together. Purlapa can also be held without dancing, in which case the men sit in an inner compact circle and women and children sit around the outside. Purlapa are infrequently held nowadays but there are some Warlpiri men keen to revitalise these ceremonies, sometimes through engagement with photos and sound and video recordings from the past.

When Baptist missions were set up in Yuendumu and Lajamanu in the 1950s, purlapa related to Christian stories about Easter and Christmas were created. Yuendumu Warlpiri people more often participate in the Easter purlapa, often travelling to Alekerenge for this ceremony at Easter time and rehearsing songs in Yuendumu for many weeks beforehand. The late Neville Japangardi Poulson explained to me that in the 1970s this purlapa was composed by a group of older men and women as a way in which they could make sense of and pass on Christian stories. Men, women and children from many different places participate in the performance of the Easter story as part of this purlapa. The songs are accompanied by rituals, theatrics and a march-like style of dancing by men and boys in which they are decorated with white fluff (traditionally down) adhered to the body with blood or sap, in a re-enactment of the Easter story. The members of the Baptist Church in Yuendumu are extremely proud of the Easter purlapa and showcase it to Christian visitors to the settlement as an example of how their Warlpiri culture has incorporated Christianity.

Warlpiri men also hold yilpinji ceremonies, often called 'love songs' or 'love magic', and like their female version, their purpose is to make people sexually attractive. These songs and the intimate ceremonies are targeted at a particular person and the singing is directed to an item of their clothing. As they sing this item of clothing is said to become 'shiny' – an attractive quality associated with red ochre and extreme beauty. When a certain person sees the person for whom yilpinji was sung wearing the piece of clothing they become attracted to them. These ceremonies are private and restricted to men only, though there are a number of yilpinji that can be sung openly as they are important for establishing the connections that Warlpiri men have to particular Country and ancestral stories.

While there is often concern among the more general Australian public about whether men's ceremonies held across the Central Desert are open or whether important cultural restrictions may be breached, the reality is that senior men have long held intricate systems for managing access to levels of knowledge surrounding ceremonies. The ceremonies are too powerful to not be managed carefully in this way and senior men's authority on these matters must be respected.

SORRY BUSINESS – FUNERAL CEREMONIES

Sadly, as is the case in many Central Australian communities, Sorry Business immediately following a death is a far too frequent ceremonial context. For Warlpiri people, the women's high-pitched wail is often an audible cue that someone has just passed away. White pipe clay is haphazardly swiped across all community members' foreheads as they prepare to go to a Sorry ground where the immediate family has gathered to mourn and receive other mourners. Families come from all over, regardless of the enormous distances they have to travel. Sorry Business cannot be finished until everyone had come and hugged the immediate female family members over the swag roll containing the deceased's blankets.

Unlike across the Top End of Australia where most communities focus their singing and dance traditions around funeral ceremonies, Central Desert Sorry Business has no songs or dance. It is a sombre event in which ritualised accusations of the cause of death are common. It is rarely accepted that a death could be a result of natural causes, even old age, and these ceremonial gatherings can be tense and often result in significant conflict. It is vital to finish 'Sorry' before the close family of a deceased person can leave the Sorry ground, which may mean that they often camp there for weeks. Christian-style funeral ceremonies of a particular Warlpiri type are held months later. While Sorry Business is a private and emotional ceremonial context where normally photographic images would be inappropriate, following the police shooting of young Warlpiri man Kumunjayi Walker in 2019, images of Sorry paint have been used for purposes of protest and to bring attention to the deep effects that this event and the many others like it across First Nations Australia have to community wellbeing.

5

ADAPTION AND EVOLUTION

WESLEY ENOCH

The year is 2009, I'm at the Garma Festival in north-east Arnhem Land at a site called Gulkula. This is an annual festival run by the Yolŋu people through the Yothu Yindi Foundation at around the beginning of August. It is a legacy of the award-winning band Yothu Yindi and their successful music career and is one of the major events dedicated to the promotion of Yolŋu culture and storytelling, influence and leadership. Garma has become a beacon for leaders of all sorts to attend to listen and talk. Prime ministers, as I wrote about in Chapter 2, government ministers, TV personalities, journalists, corporate leaders, Aboriginal leaders and many more make the trek to the Northern Territory to deliver announcements and listen to the discussions about what is being said and done there.

On this occasion, the event of the afternoon is the investiture of a respected Elder who was named as part of the Australia Day Honours List.[1] Here to officiate is the Administrator of the Northern Territory (the equivalent of a state governor); the gathering is thronging with Elders and celebrities, festival goers and family members. An investiture is a ceremony where the official welcomes the recipient, reads a citation and presents a medal and certificate. But there is something different about this event. Between the announcement on Australia Day and the Garma Festival, the recipient has died.

As we have discussed, it would be normal for the family to banish the saying of the Elder's name and all traces of them would be embargoed until a formal grieving period was fully observed, but today there will be something different on display as part of this ceremony. Something so unusual many of the gathering are confused by what exactly is happening.

The ceremony starts on the buŋgul ground (a dance ground made up of a large circle of sand, perhaps 30 metres in diameter). Family members painted in the colours of yellow and white dance and sing, carrying branches of leaves. The dancing is animated and steady, and then as a group they form a tight circle, continuing the singing, and come forward to the edge of the buŋgul ground, approaching the Administrator and the official party. The dancing group comes to a halt and the Administrator is injected into the centre of the tight clutch of family members. The singing stops. The Administrator speaks into a microphone: 'Ladies and Gentlemen.

It is my privilege to invest those people or persons who received awards in the Australia Day 2009 Honours List.'

Standing or sitting outside of the circle, you can hear the words but you can't see what is happening. The citation is read out and the name of the recipient is partially mentioned. The medal is passed to a family member and the Administrator says a few words concluding: '... and I hope people get a lot of happiness out of this recognition'.

With all their duties done, the Administrator and the official party are ejected from the tight circle and the singing starts again. Those in the circle inch their way back out to the centre of the buŋgul ground and after a while fall to their knees, slapping the ground with the leaves and raising the sand in dust clouds. And with that done, the family leave the dance ground, walking casually off to the edges.

As an observer it was hard to understand the significance of what had occurred, but later when it was explained to me I understood that perhaps I had witnessed an example of cultural adaption and evolution.

It is indeed the norm for the deceased to be recognised with a period of mourning by the family that includes not saying their name or displaying their image, but on this occasion something different had happened. Apparently the family had decided that the awarding of the Order of Australia was a proper and good thing and so they brought in a ceremony that would allow this to occur. The dancing and singing, though outside of my comprehension, were explained as an invocation of the spirits so powerful that the name could be mentioned and investiture could be held. These spirits acted as protectors and were firmly held inside the circle, with the family of dancers becoming a shield to make sure the spirits were not disturbed by outside observers. Then when the investiture was finished the dancers took the spirits back out to the sand circle and placed them into the ground. This was seen to be so powerful that even hours later the discarded branches used in the dancing were thought to be untouchable and guarded so that children and the uninitiated didn't happen upon them and become sick.

FIRST NATIONS CULTURES ARE DYNAMIC

First Nations cultures are not static or unresponsive to the world around us. Quite the opposite; there are natural adaptive mechanisms built into ceremonies that maintain integrity while incorporating the changing landscape, new stimuli and modern technologies. It is this idea of cultural adaption and evolution that has helped First Nations people evolve and adapt to become the longest continuous culture in human history, and culturally shift and change in our contemporary society. First Australians negotiate the traditional and the contemporary in everyday life and have systems that help us to absorb intrusions into our cultural life. In many ways the words 'traditional' and 'contemporary' are seen in a binary manner, but looking at their true meanings, 'traditional' refers to the intergenerational transfer of knowledge through repetition, and 'contemporary' means the here and now. Often we talk of traditional and contemporary as being antithetical to each other but, in fact, tradition only continues if it is being practiced in a contemporary manner.

There are still many who think that 'real' Aboriginal cultures are those that are not influenced by Western society; that have somehow escaped the influence of modernity. This attitude places our living culture in a glass box on a pedestal in a museum – unchanging, untouched and by extension fossilised and dead. This approach disallows cultural evolution and in many ways places our people in a bind to prove our identity by criteria that are not relevant. Using the same misconception, all English people should be still dressing like Shakespeare, Italians should be wearing togas, and all Japanese should wear kimonos to work. It is ridiculous when you think about it. How can a whole culture exist in a modern world and be expected not to find ways to use new technologies, engage with new events and generally exchange with visitors in their country. As the world changes so do all cultures and their ways of expression; some things are relegated to history, some continue unchanged, and others shift to accommodate the new.

I was taught that all the stories that were ever going to be told, every song and dance, every act of creation that was ever going to be made for all of time was created at the beginning of time itself. The act of creation of all things was a complete and fulsome act. This idea says there is no such thing as original thought or inspired creation by humans; everything from the beginning of time to the end of time has already been created by the creator and Ancestral Beings. At the time of creation these stories and dances, songs and paintings were placed in the landscape and could be resurrected when needed. There is a concept embodied in First Nations cultures that anthropologist WEH Stanner called 'everywhen',[2] in which all time is accessible at any time, that the past, present and future coexist in all places. This concept means there is nothing entirely new in the world and anything unfamiliar or that currently does not have a known story will have a story embedded in the landscape that only needs to be 'remembered'.

Ceremonies are about making sense of the world around us; they give us the knowledge of where we come from and help navigate a future. Literally, ceremonies can tell the story of how everything came into being and what our relationship is to the world as it is now. If things don't have a story yet then it is beholden on you to 'remember' the story of this object, animal, event, etc.

I was told the story of the coming of the Toyota, which was of a person seeing the tyre tracks in the sandy soil and following them to discover what made them. When they saw the vehicle they quickly told the story of the return of the serpent and its ancestral role in creation and its ability to carry people long distances. Similarly, there is a mechanism to incorporate the story of the horse, money, or anything that was not present before European arrival, into the ceremonies, songs and dancers as if they are part of the cultural tradition of a people. There is an aeroplane dance performed in the Tiwi Islands that documents the Japanese bombing of Darwin in 1942, during World War II.[3] The dancers hold their arms outstretched to represent the planes, while other dancers perform looking through binoculars and eventually shooting down the planes.

I was also told a story of a trip across the desert in the back of a Toyota Troopcarrier with a group of Aboriginal women who were singing as they were driven along. The women sang faster as they sped along the road. When the anthropologist asked why the women were singing so fast the translator said that if they did not sing up the Country, the land would not appear up over the horizon. Their songs were holding the land together and needed to be sung at a speed that would keep pace with the car. The songs were a way of navigating through the landscape. Originally designed for a walking pace, they were adapted to respond to faster modes of transport. The songs document the pathways of Ancestral Beings and the creation of topographic features. They also talk to ideas of law and the lessons learnt from the stories of creation, and as the speed of travel evolved so too did the need to adapt, to be sung faster.

Being an oral tradition means First Nations cultures are constantly being reiterated and recreated each time they are expressed. The person telling the story is simultaneously recalling the previous time they heard or performed it while making sure it is alive today, responding to the modern world. Keeping the culture alive while also observing the demands of what has gone before. There could be allegations of inconsistency or manipulation of the story by the storyteller, but it is amazing how effective the structure of song and image-based poetry is for remembering content.

Other examples of remembering long stories and instruction have been globally documented as a way of maintaining oral traditions through patterns and poetry. For millennia Nordic long-form poetry documented the creation stories of Scandinavian society and are legendary for the way they keep alive huge tracts of oral traditions through constant reciting. The telling of some stories could go for days, recalling in detail the exploits of mythic leaders all without being written down, relying instead on the memory of the trained storytellers. Think about how you can recite a poem you learnt years ago at school or how actors remember Shakespeare. There is something in the structure of the patterns of words and rhymes that helps commit the song/story to memory.

In 1999, the Queensland Theatre Company staged Shakespeare's *The Tempest*, which demonstrated the fluidity and power of adaptation. This production was directed by Simon Phillips and featured a postcolonial reading of the play where the spirits of the island were First Nations dance group Jagera Jarjum, Ariel was a Torres Strait Islander performer and Caliban an Aboriginal man. The notion of Prospero being shipwrecked on this island and learning the 'magic' of the place, enslaving the inhabitants and generally fuelling resentment and the characters' calls for freedom paralleled the story of colonial Australia. As part of the play, the dancers would appear and disappear as spirits of the island and at one point the play asks for there to be a 'masque', a moment of storytelling performed by the spirits that ends abruptly. Jagera Jarjum chose to dance an invocation for spirits to rise up. It was powerful and important to the way the show was conceived as a commentary on white–black relations, but when the 'masque' was interrupted by Prospero and the spirits – the dancers – needed to disappear, the dance remained unfinished.

During rehearsals no one questioned the logic of the play and what was being performed, but when it came to staging the curtain call, the members of Jagera Jarjum said they could not take a bow like the other actors because their performance was not finished. Again this stance was left unquestioned by the remainder of the cast, and the production team took the decision at face value, not wanting to insult the dancers and their cultural contribution. It wasn't until the previews when an audience was present that we witnessed the dancers leave the stage and race back to their dressing room, remaining fully dressed while other performers changed out of costume and left the theatre. In the dressing room after the play, Jagera Jarjum would sing at the TV monitor, which was showing the empty stage as the audience was leaving the auditorium. This was a completion of the song and a returning of the spirits to where they belong. By singing to the TV monitor the dancers had acquitted their cultural obligations. Like the Garma experience, something had been evoked and the required remedy was found to protect the audience and the rest of the cast. After a few days of this happening, Ian McDonald, the musical director, was engaged to talk through the ways the production could assist with this process. Then, through these negotiations Jagera Jarjum decided to record their singing so that it could be played in the auditorium at the end of the show. Audience members walked out of the theatre listening to the song that was protecting them and bringing the ceremony of the dance to an end.

This example shows how new technologies were engaged to complete cultural obligations, first by the idea of singing to a TV monitor in the dressing room instead of singing and dancing live on the stage to complete the cultural ceremonial protocol, and then recording the singing and playing the recording as a legitimate way to lay the spirits to rest. This is a kind of cultural gymnastics and adaption that demonstrates how cultures evolve in the face of new technologies to achieve ceremonial outcomes. There is not a form of cultural apartheid where the new cannot engage with the ancient, but rather a free-flowing, guided process of evolution.

During COVID-19 lockdowns we used video conferencing to fulfill the cultural obligation of attending funerals, however this has been around for decades. In the 1980s and 90s the use of radio broadcast through the BRACS (Broadcasting for Remote Aboriginal Communities Scheme) enabled communities to use broadcast technologies to send and receive images, programs and radio signals. As a result, the communities also found ways to incorporate these technologies into their cultural practices and ceremony, such as funerals, enhancing greater participation for those people who were isolated because of health care, incarceration, schooling or employment. These and other technologies have been used to enable cultural continuity and connection with community in the modern era.

There are so many examples of how technology is playing a role in the continuity and modernity of First Nations cultural expression. The young women who print T-shirts with the body markings needed to dance a particular song rather than go bare breasted in public, the websites promoting First Nations businesses and trade of artefacts and ochres, the accessing of block-chain technology to prove the authenticity of a painting through QR codes, the creation of NFTs (non-fungible tokens) for First Nations artistic economic development, and using augmented reality (AR) to explore untold stories of sacred sites and objects.

On Yugambeh Country near the Gold Coast there is a powerful adaptation occurring where Aunty Mary Graham and Elders of the

Kombumerri families are creating a project acknowledging the need for people to have a sense of transition from youth to adulthood. Called the Rites of Passage Project, it is a modern initiation that sets up skills and tests that help young people who graduate from the project to function more fully in community life and to take on roles in the community through strengthening cultural knowledge and skills. These include language, dance, ceremonial and cultural practices, reading the land, hunting skills and how to represent their community at public events. The Rites of Passage Project imparts values and philosophies that are connected to long traditions. The young people go through a ceremony of graduation that marks a moment of maturation, which helps them recognise their growth and validates that growth in the eyes of the community and family.

The project grew from Elders recognising the destructive behaviours that can occur when people don't value ceremony. For many, testing the boundaries of the law, civil disobedience or even going to gaol is seen as a modern initiation that marks the transition into adulthood. Adapting the old ways for the contemporary world gives meaning to those living with the pressures of modernity. In a society where Aboriginal young people are more likely to go to gaol than they are to go to university, there is a great deal of focus on constructive ways to build more meaning and find ways forward.

I did some work in juvenile detention in the 1990s where the bulk of the inmates were First Nations kids. I was engaged as a theatre teacher to run a program of activities with the objective to help them build communication and social skills. There were times when the classes went well and other days when they ended in lockdowns and confiscation of art supplies. The participants wanted mostly to play games and compete against each other. For a group of socially maladjusted kids I was surprised when they responded well to games because they liked the rules and the order, and they could win at something. They also liked simple play at a level that was perhaps suited more to kids five years younger than they were. On one occasion I decided to do a practical exercise where we built a cubby house out of bed sheets and twine. This simple structure encouraged cooperation and communication, and on its completion I could see the sense of achievement on their faces. When we entered the space and sat around under the white cotton sheet, I asked them to tell stories of themselves and their families when they were young kids. In a vain hope that they felt safe in the 'home' they had built, I was inviting them to christen the space with celebratory stories that validated their childhood.

There was silence.

'What do you mean, sir?'

'Is there a story you remember from your childhood? Maybe a family story? Something a parent or an uncle may have told you?' I was imagining a story that evoked meaning and cultural resonance for them.

'I know, sir.'

'Go on.'

'When I did my crime I made it onto page 3 of the paper.'

'Oh, that's nothing. When they nicked me I was on the TV, they all said they heard my name on the TV.'

'When I absconded [I remember how they used that official word] I was all over the TV and papers and radio.'

It struck me really clearly. These young people had a need for story and ceremony, they had a need to understand the world around them that had in many ways left them behind. But in the absence of ceremony, they sought recognition in destructive ways and asserted their story onto the public storytelling of the nation via newspapers and television. Their need to be heard had not been satisfied through tradition, nor had they found solace in the cultural practices they may or may not have been subject to. Without a sense of ceremony these young kids were perpetually striking out at the world that held no meaning for them.

I left that day thinking that ceremony and the telling of stories create the most important tool for understanding the world around us, putting into context our long history of cultural practice within the disruption of colonial interference. In the absence of story and ceremony we will make our own, so great is the need. As a result, much of the disadvantage and trauma experienced in our community can be traced back to these moments of broken connection and the inability to adapt or evolve cultural practice. Ceremony is inherently a positive and constructive endeavour but for those who don't find the cultural continuity, who don't find the way through the negotiation of the past and present and future, there is only the angry railing against things, the self-destructive and community-destructive behaviours. This experience showed me that storytelling and ceremony play a role in being a contemporary traditional Blackfella.

6

CEREMONY AS A POLITICAL ACT

WESLEY ENOCH

Ceremony has the power to change the course of history and affect the hearts and minds of those who take part.

On 26 January 1938, over one thousand Aboriginal people gathered at Sydney Town Hall at the beginning of what was called the Day of Mourning. They had come from all over the country to protest the 150 years since the arrival of the First Fleet and the beginning of the British colony in Australia. While many other Australians enjoyed parades, sailing regattas and a re-enactment of the landing of Arthur Phillip, these mourners dressed in black silently marched through the streets of Sydney, from Town Hall to Australian Hall in Elizabeth Street.

The organisers of the landing re-enactment had tried to entice local Aboriginal people to participate in it, but the community had refused to dress in lap-laps, carry spears and take part. So, instead, the organisers trucked in a group of men from western New South Wales, who they proceeded to house in the stables of the Redfern Police Barracks before dropping them at Farm Cove and instructing them to run away from the First Fleet as if scared.

By contrast, the organisers of the Day of Mourning had requested to hold their meeting in Sydney Town Hall but were rejected, so they booked Australian Hall. It is recorded that despite their booking they still had to use the back door to enter the building. Once inside they held a meeting and moved the following resolution.

> We, representing The Aborigines of Australia, assembled in conference at the Australian Hall, Sydney, on the 26th day of January, 1938, this being the 150th Anniversary of the Whiteman's seizure of our country, Hereby make Protest against the callous treatment of our people by the whitemen during the past 150 years, and we appeal to the Australian nation of today to make new laws for the education and care of Aborigines, we ask for a new policy which will raise our people to full citizen status and equality within the community.[1]

This moment is considered to be the first national Aboriginal protest to raise awareness and table demands to be recognised.

AUSTRALIA DAY

Australia Day is another example of a ceremony, but it means different things to different people. In this chapter we will unpack the origins of this ceremony, its meaning for the nation and how ceremony can be a political act.

Australia Day was not historically held on 26 January. In fact, the first Australia Day was held on 30 July 1915, and commemorated with a series of World War I fundraising activities. Subsequently, it was held on Friday 28 July 1916; Friday 27 July 1917; and Friday 26 July 1918. This was in the era of cash pay packets, which were handed out on a Thursday, and one can assume that Fridays were the best days to collect pledges and donations. With the usual Australian pragmatism, the date changed to whatever suited the cause. The ceremony was one of patriotism connected to the war effort and supporting the men and women who were protecting the Empire. You have to remember that Australia didn't exist as a country until 1901, and World War I represented a significant moment of loss and bonding for the new nation.

There are reasons why ANZAC Day ceremonies have such deep roots in the culture of Australia. The major loss of life and the effect of those soldiers who returned physically and psychologically scarred, reminded many of the sense of sacrifice and commitment to the idea of a country. Aboriginal and Torres Strait Islander men and women were not recognised as full citizens of Australia in 1915, with many not able to vote, own land, marry or travel without permission, or join the Australian Imperial Force (AIF), which the

Australian Army was called then. The rules stated that you had to be substantially European to join the AIF and so many of our people were formally rejected. However, due to their cleverness and by bending the rules, some of our men enlisted and served even if they were not recorded in the official record books as Aboriginal and/or Torres Strait Islander. It is only in the past two decades that we can prove that over 1500 Indigenous men served in World War I, but we suspect many, many more went to war although their correct details were not recorded.

With the end of the war, there was a sense that our newly traumatised 'Infant' nation needed a national day, alongside our national capital, national currency, the beginnings of our national War Memorial and other founding paraphernalia to mark our nationhood. There is an idea that to be a nation you must have ceremonies, traditions and monuments to prove it exists. The people of postwar Australia were overcome with imperial spirit and wanted to express strong bonds to our colonial history, believing a national day must reflect the narrative of King and Country, Empire and colonialism.

Around 1930, the oddly named Australian Natives' Association (ANA) advocated the adoption of 26 January as an appropriate date for the National Day. The Australian Natives' Association was open only to Australian-born white men. I can speculate that the impending 150th anniversary of the arrival of the First Fleet, in 1938, was a motivator to celebrate the colonial history and reassert the role of Australia in the British Empire. However, 26 January was a contentious date even then because it was the Foundation Day for

New South Wales and many of the other states resisted endorsing this date. A foundation day is the formal date when statehood was awarded to what was previously a colony. For Queensland it is 6 June, Western Australia it is 2 June, Tasmania is 13 September, and in South Australia it is 28 December or the first weekday after the Christmas Day holiday so as to extend the number of days off you get.

But the resistance gave way to acceptance and some of the first Australia Days were held but not on 26 January. Instead, the last Monday of January was chosen, to ensure there was a long weekend. Some records call this day ANA Day in recognition of the group that founded it.

Australia Day was just three years old when the first Indigenous protests occurred, with the instigation of the Day of Mourning in 1938. On this day, Indigenous Australians and their supporters marked the impact of colonisation, demanded full rights as citizens and mourned the loss of life in their communities with marches, talks and a resolution. After decades of petitions and regional protests, 26 January 1938 was chosen as the most appropriate date to call attention to the Australian experience, to question Australian identity and to shine a light on our history from an Indigenous perspective. Just a day earlier, on 25 January 1938, Prime Minister Joseph Lyons met with delegates from the Day of Mourning to hear their grievances. But the story goes that Lyons' primary motivation was to meet the famous young VFL footballer and organiser Doug Nicholls, who at that time was in the final year of his groundbreaking playing career. Whatever the truth, the fact is that on the day before

SECTION OF ABORIGINAL MEETING in Australian Hall, Sydney, organised by Aborigines' Progressive Association mourners.

Meeting in Australian Hall, Sydney, organised by the Aborigines' Progressive Association mourners. Aborigines Day of Mourning, 26 January 1938. Photographed by Russell Clark.

the 150th anniversary of the arrival of the First Fleet, the leader of the country sat down to talk with First Nations leaders.

The Day of Mourning has been marked each year since. So it is correct to say that Australia Day is not much older than the Indigenous protests that have accompanied every annual national day since 1938. This national public ceremony of political protest – including marches, speeches, art and music – has grown ever since. In fact, the modern-day NAIDOC (National Aborigines and Islanders Day Observance Committee) Week has its roots in the 1938 Day of Mourning.[2] The Day of Mourning or Aborigines Day was held on the Sunday before every Australia Day from 1940. In 1955, the National Aborigines Day Observance Committee decided to move the event to July and for it to become a celebration of resistance, survival and culture, rather than be a protest in response to the colonially sympathetic date. Then in the 1991, NADOC became NAIDOC in recognition of our Torres Strait Islander brothers and sisters.

This ceremony of political protest continued throughout most of the 20th century, remembering that Australia Day did not happen on 26 January each year but was held on the last Monday of January. Far from being a ceremonial occasion, many people chose to use the Australia Day long weekend to have barbeques and head to the beach. It marked the end of the summer holidays and generally lacked any structured ceremony. Since 1960, the Australian of the Year Awards have been celebrated on Australia Day, and in later years citizenship ceremonies were added on that day. But for many years, the day lacked national ritual and ceremony. By contrast, Indigenous Australians and our allies were marching and creating events of cultural significance from the 1930s on.

January has continued to inspire First Nations protest and action. Leading up to the 1967 referendum, which gave First Nations people full rights under Commonwealth law, 26 January was used to educate and celebrate, protest and show our resilience. On 26 January 1972, another high-level ceremony was created with the installation of the Aboriginal Tent Embassy on the lawns of Parliament House, Canberra. In the way of all ceremonies, the Aboriginal Tent Embassy was a strong enacting of cultural rites and traditions, and an assertion of identity. From the time the Embassy first took shape, street theatre, dance, art, speeches and marches have been held there, and a ceremonial fire has been burning there for over fifty years. In many ways the Aboriginal Tent Embassy continues to convey the demands of 1938, protesting the government's approach to Indigenous Land Rights, and promoting ideas of self-determination and sovereignty.

Ceremonies take many shapes. We have written about rites of passage, memory making, diplomacy, trade, healing and personal ceremonies. The key to ceremony is about the repetition and passing down of knowledge from one generation to another. I am arguing that the protests around Australia Day are just as much a ceremony as initiations, dances, marriages and funerals. If we accept that ceremony is a set of cultural expressions that help memorialise, shift, transition or allow exchange between groups, then protests can be seen in this light. When we use gatherings, arts and ritual to express ourselves, then can't we say that First Nations political protests are a continuation of ceremonial purpose? It is too easy for others to see political protests as modern and not ceremonial, but as Aboriginal people we are in charge of what we call ceremony. We can have ceremonies that are continuations of age-old traditions, and we can find new ceremonies that express who we are today with no lack of validity. Protests have become ceremonial through the repeated actions being passed down through families over a great span of time. The protests and other events surrounding 26 January by First Nations people (and allies) have become a parallel ceremony to the 'official' ceremonies held and watched by the Australian nation. Music festivals such as Yabun, held annually on 26 January in Sydney, and other Survival Day-badged events have become commonplace and a tradition passed down over many decades. It has become tradition to use public events to help profile our cause and make public ceremonial spaces for our Voice to be heard.

This was clearly articulated in 1982 at the Brisbane Commonwealth Games, where protesters marched to bring attention to the colonial history of the Games and the country. The idea of the 'Stolenwealth Games' campaign was started, using the international media presence to raise the issues of Land Rights and the control of Aboriginal affairs, highlighting injustices and protecting Country from mining. In 1978, the Queensland Premier Joh Bjelke-Petersen actually made marches and demonstrations illegal. Later, in the 1980s, these laws were used to dampen the criticism of the Games and were an attempt to stop Aboriginal and Torres Strait Islander people from exercising what has become a traditional practice. The Sydney Olympic Games in 2000, the 2006 Melbourne Commonwealth Games and the 2018 Gold Coast Commonwealth Games were all accompanied by marches and protest. The evolution of these protests and public ceremonies, though loud and disruptive, were never intended to be violent, although violence was sometimes a byproduct of police intervention. Uncle Dennis Walker famously wore a motorcycle helmet to the demonstrations in the 1970s to protect his head from bludgeoning by police. On most occasions marches were peaceful affairs to highlight the visibility of First Nations people and our issues.

Back to Australia Day, and by the time the bicentenary of the arrival of the First Fleet came around in 1988, terms such as 'Survival Day' and 'Invasion Day' were in common usage. The Day of Mourning gave way to a narrative of survival against the colonial history, and with a contradictory backdrop of the 'Celebration of a Nation' thousands of people descended again on the streets of Sydney to march and demonstrate First Nations' resilience. Not only in Sydney but across Australia there was a questioning of the relevance of the date as a national day. In 1988, the country was reminded that it was still celebrating a colonial past, a past that did not reflect the establishment of the nation (that in fact was 1 January 1901). It was celebrating the arrival of the First Fleet and the formal beginning of the British colony.

In 1988, the tradition of an Australia Day long weekend was temporarily changed. The public holiday was held on a Tuesday to coincide with the 26th, and for most Australians the change was fine – they took an extra-long long weekend. With bicentennial celebrations lasting the whole of 1988, this exuberant investment in national identity started the ball rolling for a permanent change. Governments thought that if we were going to have a national day we should have it on the actual day. By 1994, the states and territories unified under a national public holiday to be held on 26 January.

That's right! It has only been since 1994 that we have annually observed Australia Day on the 26th. I raise this because it says something about the lack of ritual and ceremony of Australia Day. As a long weekend the traditions and ceremonies were underdeveloped. The rituals were, arguably, having a barbecue and a few drinks with friends, jingoistic nationalism, weird re-enactments, fireworks, ferry races, demonstrations of military hardware, driving around with an Australian flag hanging out the back window, and, until recently, the Triple J Hottest 100 (in 2017 they decided to change the date). For the lucky few, there are genuine events on this day in the naturalisation ceremonies, where those who have recently arrived become citizens of Australia. In modern days we have developed the Australian of the Year Awards in 1960, and the announcement of the Australia Day Honours List from 1975 on; in Sydney there is the WugulOra Morning Ceremony, telecast nationally, where officials acknowledge the start of Australia Day and local Aboriginal people perform. This ceremony is a heartfelt response to the need to acknowledge First Nations people and the role we play in the history of this continent.

At least today we have the tradition of the lamb ads released around 26 January to look forward to!

Noel Pearson says there are three narratives that make Australia: the story of the longest continuous living culture on Earth; the tale of the British colonial project and the institutions that have helped shape our society; and the narrative of the most successful multi-ethnic, multicultural nation on the planet.[3] Every time we walk down the street, we see these three narratives unambiguously intertwined. The influence of the Westminster form of representative democracy, the judiciary, Indigenous knowledge, history, people, our landscape, the faces of our friends and families, the food we eat, the languages we hear and speak. These narratives are inescapable. But for some Australians, these narratives seem to be in conflict, antithetical to each other, and these people seek a world where one dominates the others to prove a superiority. This battle flares most significantly in the weeks leading up to 26 January – the questions around who owns the date, what it means and what we do on the day that makes us Australian.

I think these tensions arise because the rituals and ceremonies we have developed are not reflecting the truth of who we are as a modern nation. For guidance, we can look to our other national commemoration, ANZAC Day, which is a much older and clearer example of how we could shape a day that tells the story of our country. And how we tell these stories matters. On 25 April, we start with a dawn service full of poetry, music, symbolism, a minute's silence, quiet reflection and a sense of the dawn of a new day; followed by a march where we pay respect to those who have served, consider the human price of war and the sacrifice of family members. That's followed by family gatherings and old mates sharing some time together to yarn, exchange stories and memories, a trip to a pub, and a game of two-up. Over time, ANZAC Day has developed traditions and commemorations that can access great pain, show respect and after an appropriate sense of ceremony, celebrate life and survival and peace through a party.

The date 26 January represents the beginning of the British project on this continent and has come to embody the constant debate about those early colonial days and the relationship with First Nations people. Gadigal Land and Sydney have become a flash point for several types of ceremonial events, from theatre shows, protests, music festivals, installations and oratorio.

Jane Harrison in her play *The Visitors* takes us back to 26 January 1788, and we listen to a fictionalised conversation between local Elders about the arrival of the British ships and the idea of cultural protocol – should the visitors be welcomed as is customary or should they be rejected due to the threat they pose? It is a powerful evocation of conflicting ceremonies and a sense of how the world could have been different.

There is a movement to take a day of reflection before the Australia Day public holiday. At the Sydney Festival they hold *The Vigil*, which is an event on the evening of 25 January that invites people to gather and consider the day before the arrival of the First Fleet – what life and the country would have been like before everything changed. As on 25 January in 1938, when the Prime Minister of the day sat with First Nations leaders and talked about their demands, *The Vigil* has the possibility to grow into a new tradition of respect and listening.

It is worth looking at ceremony as political action that is overt, such as public demonstrations and marches, and the more covert political action of experiential and participatory art projects. Both are ways of affecting policy makers and changing the hearts and minds of the country. Another Sydney Festival event, held in 2018, was the participatory art installation *Four Thousand Fish* at Barangaroo, curated by Kalari (south-west New South Wales) woman Emily McDaniel. It was a response to the story of early colonists in Sydney who had netted 4000 fish from the harbour. This was seen as a sign of greed by local Aboriginal people and disrupted the fish stocks. After taking far more than was needed to feed the colony, the British then distributed the fish among the Aboriginal men, undermining the role of women in fishing and feeding families. During the art project people were encouraged to fill fish moulds with water from Sydney Harbour and freeze it. They then would take a 'frozen fish' and place it in a canoe made of metal and let it melt back into the harbour as a symbol of returning the wasted fish and acknowledging the past.

Though these projects might not have been overtly political, it is fair to say they were ceremonial responses to the need to educate and heal the country through storytelling.

One example of overt political action as ceremony was the Walk for Reconciliation on 28 May 2000. Over 250,000 people walked across the Sydney Harbour Bridge, and elsewhere around the nation hundreds of thousands walked in the name of Reconciliation as a symbolic gesture of bridging the divide between First Nations and non-First Nations people. The previous day, at the Corroboree 2000 gathering at the Sydney Opera House, highlighted as a ceremonial gathering of Australians to make commitments to reconciliation in the lead up to the centenary of Federation, Prime Minister John Howard rejected the idea of apologising to the Stolen Generations. There was a great deal of dismay and hurt, with many people in the room standing and turning their backs on the Prime Minister during his speech. The subsequent Apology to the Stolen Generations delivered by Prime Minister Kevin Rudd to Federal Parliament on 13 February 2008 was a massive healing ceremony for many survivors of the government policy of forced removal of children from their families. The power of recognition is a way in which a political action can be ceremony for the nation.

Not all ceremonies for First Nations people push against the colonial history of the nation. In the Torres Strait there is a ceremony connected to the coming of Christianity to the islands. Called The Coming of the Light, it revolves around the anniversary of the arrival on Erub Island of Reverend Samuel MacFarlane from the London Missionary Society on 1 July 1871. The Coming of the Light is remembered with a public holiday on the islands and commemorated with a series of church services, feasts and dance. For the outsider it may seem antithetical to First Nations values to accept a colonising influence such as Christianity, but stories abound of warring and retribution throughout the islands in the years leading up to the arrival of the Church. Depending on which histories you listen to, there were devastating wars where Islanders would attack each other regularly, to the point where people on some islands were threatened with extinction. These attacks would then inspire retribution where relatives on neighbouring islands would conduct raids on the aggressor in a cycle of existential violence. The arrival of Christianity with its narrative of forgiveness and love came at an important moment for the Torres Strait and helped heal rifts and divisions. The ceremony attached to the Christian Church assisted people to find unity and peace and is remembered to this day as a positive moment in the development of Torres Strait Island culture.

The most recent sense of ceremony as politics can be observed in the Uluṟu Statement from the Heart (included at the end of this book) and the subsequent Yes campaign. Prior to the Uluṟu First Nations Constitutional Convention in 2017, regional dialogues were held around the country and thousands of First Nations people took part in discussions and debate about the needs of our people. There were ceremonies of truth-telling and making space so participants could have their say. The outcome, the Uluṟu Statement from the Heart, which was first read at the Convention on 26 May 2017, is a document and an artefact that toured the country in an attempt to persuade people about the need for constitutional change. The Statement from the Heart asks for a Makarrata or a ceremonial process of coming together after a struggle to find truth and peace.

In many ways the throughline of all these ceremonies as political action is the need for justice and truth and respect for the power of the First Nations of this country. Almost all First Nations political action is a response to 26 January in terms of what it represents and the legacy of the dispossession that followed. The Yes campaign and referendum were a ceremony on a massive national scale, where Australians were asked to participate in changing the foundation document of the country to correct the falsehoods of the past and map out a new future. Regardless of the outcome, this moment was the most important test of the power of ceremony to make a difference in our lives.

Ceremony has the power to heal individually and collectively, and First Nations people have been engaged in making ceremony for political change for a very, very long time.

7

INTERREGIONAL FESTIVALS

GEORGIA CURRAN

Many years ago, in 2006, I travelled to Kalkarinji from Yuendumu with a large group of Warlpiri women. Our convoy consisted of a bus and two troopies, both with trailers – all packed to capacity with blankets, bags, billy cans, drums of flour and ritual items required for the ceremonial exchanges that would occur in the days to come. We were unable to take the 'short cut' road through the back of Warlpiri Country due to heavy rains, so instead went around on the main road on an epic three-day journey. When we arrived we quickly overcame our travel exhaustion, as we joined hundreds of women from various communities across Central Australia. The remote bush site had been set up specifically for this event and proudly hosted by Gurindji women. The energy was buzzing! Women had come from as far east as Borroloola, from A<u>n</u>angu Pitjantjatjara Yankunytjatjara (APY) communities in the south, and from Kimberley communities in the north-west.

Each group had established their camp at a point around the ceremonial ground, which was freshly graded in preparation for a week of ceremonial singing, dancing and painting up – of holding yawulyu or awely, as this genre of women's ceremonial song is known variously across Central Australia. Our Warlpiri group from Yuendumu were enthusiastic, even dominating participants in these Women's Law and Culture meetings. Each year they were hosted by a different community, beginning in the 1990s in the Kimberley region and later becoming more focused in Central Australia due to support from the Central Land Council. Until around 2014, when they abruptly stopped due to the withdrawal of funding and support, these events were key on the annual calendars of senior women across Central Australia as being prime opportunities to get important business done.

Shortly after we arrived that evening, a number of the senior women from Yuendumu ventured out into the middle of the ceremonial ground to insert two ceremonial poles, kuturu, that our group had brought with us. Women from other communities came over to touch the kuturu and rub them with ochre and oil. A lengthy hair string, also densely soaked with red-ochre infused oil, was strung between the poles and adorned with various feathers and materials. When the senior women had finished, the rest of the women in attendance were instructed to go over to do the same – acknowledge the kuturu with respect, smooth our hands down their length and give attention to their centrality in the ceremonial activities that would take place over the following days. These ceremonial poles were the physical manifestation of the two Jangalas – Ancestral Beings central to the Warlukurlangu yawulyu – which I also participated in during my first night in Yuendumu and wrote about in Chapter 1.

I awoke the next morning, having slept in a privileged position wedged between my two close Warlpiri friends, Coral Napangardi Gallagher and Maggie Napaljarri Ross, both highly respected ceremonial leaders at the time but who have sadly since passed away. Coral had wanted us to sleep immediately alongside the ceremonial ground so she could keep watch over the kuturu during the night. She indicated to me when she saw I was awake that we should go over and touch them again to begin the day, a pattern that we continued for the rest of the week. Over that next week, different community groups showcased their ceremonial songs, flagged visually by different skirt colours. Yuendumu women, in their black skirts, used this time to get serious business done. They opened up ceremonies that had been closed due to deaths, and taught younger women their own ancestral dances so they could continue these legacies. They took advantage of the sharing of this space with women from other communities to hold business around ancestral Songlines, which connect them spiritually across countries.

These strictly female-only contexts with many key ceremonial leaders from across a wide region allowed for broader business to be held too – largely around the deaths of senior ceremonial leaders from the region. At these gatherings, the focus was for each group to showcase various songs and dances connected to particular Ancestral Beings and stories. Rather than an exchange of materials as may have been a focus of regional gatherings in the past, these events were about presenting ceremonies specific to particular communities, although certainly also influential to the other groups. They created a context for a broader sharing and set up of ceremonial connections across Central Australia, but they are not as centred on learning new materials for adoption into their performance repertories as may have been the case in exchange ceremonies of a previous era.

REGIONAL ALLIANCES AND SHARING CEREMONIAL MATERIAL

When I began writing this book I had several conversations with senior anthropologist Nicolas Peterson, who supervised my PhD research and introduced me to many of the Warlpiri families I have since worked with in Yuendumu over the years. In the 1960s and 70s, Nic spent significant time in northern and Central Australia. For nine months he lived with a self-provisioning group of men living around the south-eastern corner of the Arafura Swamp region (some of whom appear in the film *Ten Canoes*). Also, for a period in the early 1970s, Nic and his wife lived in Yuendumu and regularly participated in Warlpiri ceremonies. In his comparative work he shows that a primary reason for the widescale movements of Aboriginal groups was to participate in ceremonial gatherings requiring people from various regions. This was a much bigger preoccupation than sourcing seasonally abundant food as is often assumed, particularly for desert-based groups. Nic pointed out that it's hard to understand the structure of ceremonies held today without first understanding some of the broader ceremonial complexes that were prominent in the 1970s and 80s but have not been held in recent decades. These ceremonial complexes had many different parts and stages, which were held over many months and sometimes years. To help understand these complexes, I draw on an ethnographic description documented by the anthropologist Mervyn Meggitt, who largely worked in the northern Warlpiri settlement of Lajamanu (then called Hooker Creek) in the 1950s. This ethnography illustrates the importance placed in these past eras on keeping strong regional alliances and sharing ceremonial material – matters that remain central to First Nations festivals held across Australia today.

'RELIGIOUS FESTIVALS'

To understand the significance of current festivals it is necessary to think back to a time before the establishment of settlements across the Central Desert. Day to day, people lived in small groups of two or three families numbering around fifteen to twenty people in all. Each of these groups would have had a good idea where other people in the region were and from time to time would see their hunting fires in the flat plains. There would be considerable contact between the people who lived elsewhere in the region and the families living in these groups, with regular visits between them. When food, water and other resources were plentiful, these groups would gather for Kurdiji ceremonies, and a year or two later the young men would be put through a Kankarlu ceremony, as described in Chapter 4. These were 'religious festivals', also known as Kajirri across the Warlpiri region, which brought together 100 to 150 people. In addition to furthering the young men's ceremonial knowledge, they reflected the widest political unit where people knew and trusted one another. At these festivals groups of men from different places would share ceremonies relating to their own Country with all the other men present, and in doing so they built on their ceremonial and geographical knowledge.

Mervyn Meggitt's seminal book *The Gadjari among the Walbiri Aborigines of Central Australia*[1] is a detailed account of a no-longer held but previously important ceremonial complex or religious festival. Though known among Warlpiri groups as 'Kajirri', it is also known as 'Big Sunday' in a more regionally inclusive language across the north of Australia. Here, I will use the word and spelling Kajirri, adapting to the now standardised Warlpiri orthography. Central to the Kajirri festival is the Mamarntarrpari myth – linked to important sites along an extended Songline through Warlpiri Country and concerning the travels of exploits of Ancestral Beings focal to Warlpiri Dreaming stories. While the Mamarntarrpari myth is not the focus here, I mention it to illustrate how large-scale ceremonial complexes are intimately tied to ancestral events and honour their continuation through links to land and practices central to ancestral stories. It is easy to see the fanfare and political agendas of these grander scale ceremonies and lose sight of their embeddedness in particular ancestral stories and land. Additionally, as many ceremonial complexes, including the Kajirri, were once traded across Australia, this account shows how newly adopted ceremonial practices from other groups become relevant to local families and Aboriginal groups through the embedding of the ceremony into the ancestral stories from their own Country. The trading of a ceremony from one group to another in this way can be likened to a transfer of the intellectual property rights or copyright for that ceremony.

Up until some point in the 1980s, the exchange of ceremonial material was crucial to large-scale gatherings between Aboriginal groups. This resulted in the widespread trade of songs, dances, ritual designs and highly valued material objects, and 'religious festivals' were primary times in which these were learned and exchanged across groups. Meggitt explains how the Kajirri ceremonial complexes were adopted into Warlpiri groups from other more northern groups:

> although the Walbiri take the Gadjari rituals to be a comparatively new cultural acquisition, they regard the validating myth of the Mamandabari as dealing with events of the dreamtime just as does any other Walbiri myth.[2]

He goes on to observe that:

> on the basis of Warlbiri myth material we may infer that the Mamandabari myth and the Gadjari are not organically or

> necessarily related. The Gadjari cult complex is an importation, for which the indigenous Mamandabari myth provides a rationale that has a very different orientation from that underlying the Big Sunday further north.[3]

As mentioned in Chapter 4, ceremonies can have more than one purpose. A ceremony that may be well known in Warlpiri Country to assist with the increase of a particular plant species, for example, could also be used centrally for another functional purpose, such as to guide a young man on a further stage of his education. Similarly, a ceremonial complex that Warlpiri people have adopted for the purposes of forming regional links to other groups, can also be connected to ancestral stories from Warlpiri Country that have additional underlying purposes within themselves.

Meggitt also emphasises the clear connections that the Kajirri ceremony has to the Kunapipi ('Big Sunday') ceremony widely performed across northern Australia.[4] He understands that these connections show how this ceremony has come to Warlpiri groups from the eastern Warumunga groups (around the region of present-day Tennant Creek) and that those groups obtained it from more northern groups in Arnhem Land at an earlier time. The long distances across which ceremonies are traded and exchanged was a focus in these past eras. Many Elders today living in remote communities across the Northern Territory and Western Australia can recount trade networks for ceremonies that go back well beyond their own memories. These are vital oral histories that are told as contexts and understanding for the present-day ceremonies. This widespread exchange of ceremonial material was achieved through broad-ranging invitations to other groups from neighbouring areas that would travel long distances to attend, as well as expecting that when they sent out invitations to their own local ceremonies that other groups would reciprocate. The logistical demands of getting large numbers of people from many groups together and preparing adequate food has always been a challenging part of large-scale ceremonial events, as much today as ever – as any festival event organiser will testify! In the film *Waiting for Harry* these matters are clear as people come from long distances to hold an important funeral ceremony. The film centres on the impending arrival of a man named Harry. He is pivotal to ceremonial events but is never able to make it due to various contingences that arise on his journey. The film also explores the ways in which the ceremony has to be reorganised to manage the events without him.[5] The enormous efforts that go into organising logistics and the political tensions that surround ceremonial gatherings are testament to the value that they have in Aboriginal peoples' lives.

Stephen Wild, ethnomusicologist who worked in Lajamanu from 1969 to 1971, describes the broader significance of how ceremonial complexes like Kajirri related to positions of leadership and authority.[6] In the early days of the establishment of the Hooker Creek settlement in the late 1940s, police officers, station owners and missionaries did much to undermine traditional systems of authority, leading to decay in the existing structures of leadership. He argues that the previous complexes of ceremonial events that came together for men's initiatory rites were once quite separate affairs, but by the early 1970s they had become clumped together and performed over the six-week break of the school holidays when people were free from their other work and schooling duties. Wild indicates the importance of these shifts in noting the strict ineligibility for a man to marry prior to the Kajirri ceremony and the social ostracism that he would face if he had run off with a woman without this establishment of his right to marry. This has changed significantly in Warlpiri communities, and while Kurdiji ceremonies still set up 'promised marriages', they are more focused on creating regional alliances between families rather than an expectation of actual marriages.

In Chapter 4, the description of the two-day Kurdiji ceremonies held by Warlpiri families living in Yuendumu today shows that in recent decades these once more intimate ceremonies involving only a few family groups have expanded into large-scale affairs involving hundreds of people, travelling long distances. Kajirri has not been held since the 1980s, likely leading to the noted expansion of Kurdiji as the primary way in which boys become young men.

CURRENT FESTIVALS

The First Nations festivals that are held across Australia today in many ways share a similar focus to the widespread and readily traded structures of 'religious festivals' such as Kajirri. It is common for a particular community or mob within a city or town to take on the role of host for a festival, inviting other First Nations groups from across the country. This is the case for Yabun in Sydney, Barunga and Garma at Gulkula in the Northern Territory, and Mowanjum in Western Australia, and many others around the country. An exemplar of many First Nations festivals is the Laura Quinkan Dance Festival, held in the north Queensland town of Laura every two years. The Laura Festival began in the 1980s, making it one of the longest-running cultural festivals in the country. Its venue is the Ang-Gnarra Festival site, a respected and sacred site and home of the traditional Bora grounds. For the festival, communities from across Cape York and beyond come together to celebrate with music, dance, singing and cultural performance.[7] Also central to many other Indigenous Australian festivals are some common themes, including a long history, the important site on which it is held, regularity ensuring a future, and the opportunity for many communities to come together.

As well as these First Nations festivals there are also multicultural festivals that invite First Nations groups to perform. National and global festivals such as WOMADelaide, Perth Festival, Sydney Festival, Festival of Pacific Arts and Culture (various locations across the Pacific) are some examples of those that encourage Indigenous participation and focus on First Nations cultures as part of a regional identity. This is perhaps an important difference from the 'religious festivals' described earlier in this chapter. Nowadays, with broader audiences who may not understand the intricacies or seriousness of the religious components, there is a strong emphasis on showcasing Aboriginal cultures from different regions in a display of pride in cultural identity.

Often in festivals held today there is an emphasis on the alliances created with other groups both in the performative moments and linking back to historical ties that may or may not have been ongoing through time. An example of this is when Warlpiri women from Yuendumu performed at Barunga Festival in the Northern Territory in 2018, and specifically chose to perform the Jardiwanpa yawulyu, a Songline directly relating to ancestral stories from Warlpiri Country and further to the south; as well, it is described as having links to the north where it finishes near the sea beyond Gunbalanya (Oenpelli). Through linking this desert group to those in this more northern location at Barunga, the Warlpiri performers re-asserted this connection while also making it relevant for audiences from the Top End. In addition, the choice of this particular Songline joins together three different Warlpiri women's groups associated with Yarripiri (snake), Yankirri (emu), Ngurlu (seed) – giving all Warlpiri women who had travelled for the festival an important performance role.

These current-day festival contexts may appear to deprioritise many of the political negotiations that were central to 'religious festivals' like Kajirri, instead emphasising the individuality and uniqueness of the many different First Nations groups across Australia. Yet these festivals are profoundly political, centred on negotiations between groups, on future plans, on engagements with governments and reconciliation initiatives. These are sites set up specifically to manage the interrelations between groups, allowing space for them to assert and showcase their own cultures and positions and to strengthen relationships.

The Barunga Festival began in the 1980s with a political statement. As Bangardi man Robert Lee, champion of Jawoyn Land Rights and central to the Barunga festival set up, states: 'The main aim of the festival is to bring people together, sharing and understanding each other's problems. This is so we can get to know one another properly'.[8] The acclaimed Barunga Statement, painted during the 1988 Barunga Festival, called for Land Rights, a treaty, self-determination policies, compensation for land loss, protection of sacred sites, return of ancestral remains, linguistic and cultural rights and recognition of customary law in police and justice systems. This statement was signed off by then Prime Minister Bob Hawke, who promised but failed to deliver a treaty within two years – an act centralised in Yothu Yindi's hit song 'Treaty'. Today the Barunga Statement is in Parliament House in Canberra, where it was hung in 1991.

Garma at Gulkula is another example of a First Nations festival with a focus on contemporary politics. As Wesley noted earlier, many prominent federal and state politicians from across Australia attend the Garma Festival, as well as Indigenous spokespeople from many regions of Australia. Panel sessions are organised during the festival with discussions about major political issues pertinent to Indigenous people across Australia, and there is often live streaming and heavy reportage, as well as showcasing of Yolŋu ceremonies from the east Arnhem region.

Yabun, held yearly at Victoria Park, next to the University of Sydney, may seem to have a similar political purpose as it is held on 26 January, but it has a less formal vibe, with some ceremonial dances, bands and merchandise that are focused on celebrating First Nations cultures rather than on protest. Organisers, performers and participants are making a political statement in being there for Survival Day rather than attending the myriad of other more mainstream events held on this day.

The set up of current First Nations festivals across Australia and the readiness and excitement of many Aboriginal groups to travel long distances and engage with other First Nations groups nationally and globally have deep links to the religious festivals, such as Kajirri, which were held in the past. There are similarities in that they support long-held alliances with other Aboriginal groups across Australia, are often shaped by contemporary local, national and global political concerns, are opportunities to showcase cultural traditions with pride and in contexts where they are adequately appreciated. These festivals are also increasingly important as spaces where young First Nations people learn their own ceremonial traditions and have an opportunity to perform them today, as many of the young men at Kajirri were doing in the past.

RECLAIMING CEREMONY

In October 2024, I sat on the steps of the Sydney Opera House with my two teenage sons and pre-teen daughter, looking down onto the sand that had been brought there to form a ceremony ground for that year's DanceRites. I opened my iPhone to peruse the lineup – nineteen First Nations groups has been selected from various regions across New South Wales, from the Torres Strait Islands and Queensland, and Nyoongar groups from Perth. Many of the performers were a similar age to my own kids. The Boigu Island Kayn Kuap Dance Team was up at that moment. They had a strong group of singers and drummers as well as their dancers – their movements weren't showy or overly athletic, but their cultural strength was profound. Next up were a Bundjalung and Wiradjuri all-female group, the Buuja Buuja Butterfly Dancers. In a bold statement of cultural pride, they asserted their heritage through deft movements and well-choreographed cultural dance. The winners of this annual dance competition receive significant prize money – a matter that is always mentioned at this event despite the money being insignificant compared to the priceless feelings that come from the sharing of culture and the strength of the performers.

I thought back to the 2023 DanceRites, which was also held at the Opera House Forecourt. In the break following all the performances in the heats and while the judges were deciding on which dance groups would win the prize money and various awards, the event comperes interviewed some of the performers in front of the audience. Many of the young kids were too shy to speak on the mic – although moments before they had confidently performed for the large crowd. One young man, however, when asked what he had enjoyed most about the last two days, said that he had liked watching the other groups dancing and seeing performances from other places. Another joined in, saying that he'd liked performing himself – that he'd been watching different mobs performing for DanceRites on YouTube for years back in his community in remote south-west Queensland. This had been a strong inspiration for him to get a group together and learn these dances – reclaiming this important way of demonstrating cultural pride in front of others who were doing the same and in front of Aboriginal people from various places who understand the ceremonial power in doing so.

In June 2024, I had travelled with my Warlpiri friends and colleagues, Enid Nangala Gallagher, Marlette Napurrurla Ross and Samantha Napaljarri Watson to the Festival for Pacific Arts and Culture, held that year in Honolulu. Following a spectacular seven-hour, Olympic-style Opening Ceremony in which the Warlpiri women had joined in representing Australia, Enid and I reflected on the various ways in which the Pacific nations had chosen to represent themselves. Enid said she thought the nation that had included the most kids in their delegation was the best; her choice had nothing to do with flash costumes, fancy dance moves or virtuoso singers, which had all been on show as part of the opening event, and everything to do with assurance of cultural continuity and pride.

8

STAGING CEREMONY

GEORGIA CURRAN

The Central Land Council (CLC) organised an event at the Alice Springs Telegraph Station for their fiftieth anniversary in October 2024. Thousands attended, including people who lived in Alice Springs and many large groups that travelled in from remote communities, as well as others who came from across Australia. The celebration, which recognised the fifty-year struggle for Aboriginal rights to their land, was a major event and central to it was ceremony. As was reiterated many times throughout the evening, performances were staged to represent each of the CLC's nine subregions. These events included speeches and bands, a panel discussion with Central

Australian Aboriginal leader and previous CLC deputy chair Geoff Shaw, prominent Indigenous academic and leader Marcia Langton and former senator and Indigenous rights activist Patrick Dodson, traditional dances from Pitjantjatjara, Arrernte and Warlpiri communities, the soul-hitting voice of Mudburra woman, Eleanor Jawurlngali Dixon, and a headline act from Pitjantjatjara singer and songwriter Frank Yaama to ensure the crowd was up dancing to end the night.

The Warlpiri Southern Ngaliya Dancers from Yuendumu were invited to represent the Tanami region. During the evening, the current Chairperson of the CLC and senior Warlpiri man, Warren Japanangka Williams, talked with me about how good it is that the Warlpiri women offer such strong representation for the region, for Warlpiri communities and for Yuendumu. These kinds of staged opportunities to perform ceremony are clearly important for this broader recognition.

Around an hour before the scheduled time for their performance, the large group from Yuendumu went to the area marked off as backstage to paint up each other's chests and upper arms with elaborate ochred designs. In community contexts this is a core part of this women's business, which everyone involved knows about and participates in. Whereas in these staged contexts an audience only sees the dance at the end and none of the preparations. As the backstage paint up began, the mood rose. The beautiful descending melodic contours of yawulyu began to fill the air, soon joined by clapstick beats. I started to worry that the singing might overpower the reggae band that was currently performing on stage. With true

Warlpiri humour, especially prominent in ceremonial contexts, in the pauses between songs, one of the senior women would bust into the centre of the group with a modern 'sexy dance' style that typified the way teenagers and younger women across the Central Desert dance at rock concerts and discos and was met with laughter from the others.

When it was time, the group walked out together to the dance ground, sectioned off directly in front of the stage. The singers took their places, facing away from the audience and towards the area where the dancers would come in. Earlier that morning, the senior women of the group had had intense discussion around what would be performed that afternoon. The Ngapa 'Rain' Dreaming songs were always popular and many key owners for this Dreaming were there to lead. Two iconic verses from this Songline were chosen, showcasing the descending cyclical melodies, the poetic words set to strong rhythms and the musical pattern in which they are repeated a number of times across the performance with short breaks in between. There was also a discussion around an old film that we'd watched of Warlpiri ladies dancing Ngapa for NADOC (now NAIDOC) Week in Darwin in 1989. The women wanted to structure their performance in the same way to include a big group of both kirda (owners) and kurdungurlu (managers) – important complimentary roles in all Warlpiri ceremonial spaces (see Chapter 4). The senior women wanted to present themselves in this way, as a big and inclusive group – owners, managers, Elders, young women and kids – everyone together in one group for everyone to see. Ngapa are also public songs so there were no restrictions for the audience and the young kids could participate too. In the many accolades from the audience following this performance, there were positive comments about the large size of the group and the importance of the kids being there.

In recent years the Warlpiri women have become more and more accustomed to these kinds of 'performances' of their ceremonial songs and dances. A core group has travelled across Australia to perform at events, including festivals, theatrical productions and in many instances at conferences or other academic forums focused on our collaborative research projects.[1] Performing ceremony with the required adaptations for an audience who know very little about its background has in many ways become an expectation of what a trip away from Central Australia is all about. In 2018, I organised a group of sixteen Warlpiri men and women to travel to Canberra primarily so they could review archival audio-visual materials at AIATSIS. Soon after the group arrived, I was asked, 'Where are we going to dance?' This was quickly resolved with a visit to the Aboriginal Tent Embassy, whose residents were more than happy to host an afternoon of purlapa and yawulyu and which drew an easy crowd of family, friends and passersby.[2] This emphasised the importance of place and sites of significance, such as the Tent Embassy, to all ceremonies, past and present.

Performance opportunities for First Nations people across Australia have multiplied significantly in recent decades, as recognition and respect for the unique cultures and ceremonial traditions around the country have grown. There is a strong demand from events organisers for community group performances as part of larger events, for example (see Chapter 9). In these instances, the details of the religious significance of the songs and dances are not necessarily explained or understood by the audience. Nevertheless, the spectacle of performance, albeit with a clear and powerful social purpose, allows audiences to engage in other ways, as those watching increase their knowledge and understanding of First Nations cultures and their centrality to Australia's national identity.

Staged events often require a rethinking of the ways to present ceremonial traditions as well as consideration of the purposes for doing so. In community-focused ceremonial contexts, everyone is a participant and has appreciation for the value of the ceremony; a separate audience does not exist. In many of the festival contexts where staged versions of ceremony are showcased in front of spectators, the distinction between audience and performers is marked spatially. This may be by an actual stage or by a sectioned-off area (a ceremonial ground at a festival, for example). The audience sits at a designated distance from the singers and dancers, and this marks them as viewers. Additionally, performances are often marked by a set time slot that has a scheduled beginning and end. The participants often gauge the success of the performance by the applause and enthusiasm of the audience. The performers' cultural expertise is acknowledged and the responses seen as markers of connectedness.

As more opportunities have emerged, Warlpiri performers have often discussed ways to adapt and shape performances to engage with their audiences. In 2018, a group of Warlpiri women were invited to participate in a broader event called Unbroken Land, a promenade performance in which the audience as a group walked through a number of stages set up throughout the Alice Springs Desert Park. The audience would view a different performance at each stage, and an announcement would come through on a walkie-talkie for the performers waiting at their stage, to let them know the audience was about to arrive.

Warlpiri performers had an allocated space in the park to get ready and where they would dance, backed by a screen with printed photographs of a site on Warlpiri Country that related to the songs they were singing. The Warlpiri women were to sing the same two verses of the Ngapa ('rain') yawulyu for two audiences over three consecutive nights. By the final night they had refined the ways in which they presented these songs and adapted their performance to fit with the audience expectations and feedback. The lead dancer, Nellie Nangala Wayne, saw such a performance, which is prepared and rehearsed in advance, as an opportunity for innovation. She finished on the final night with a mimetic dance of Kirrkalanji, the name of the eagle central to the Ngapa Dreaming, in which she 'flew' close to the audience to close the performance with direct eye contact. It is unusual to see this kind of mimetic dance in Warlpiri women's yawulyu, as they more typically involve actions that depict the travels of Ancestral Beings in a rhythmically repetitive style. This innovative element being incorporated by this individual dancer (who was also a senior owner and therefore in a position of authority to make these shifts) established direct engagement with the audience.

These kinds of adaptations have led Warlpiri women to rethink the purposes for performing ceremonial songs and dances for audiences outside of Warlpiri Country. The importance of honouring Ancestral Beings and stories is always central, but the ways in which this is done adapt to these differing contexts and audiences. Barbara Napanangka Martin, one of the Warlpiri dancers, explained to a friend who had asked her about a performance event, 'We were really just showing off!' – emphasising Warlpiri women's motivations to show a broader world their ceremonial song and dance traditions and be acknowledged for the prestige of this special part of their cultural identity. Building connections to others through performances, especially in locations for which performers travel significant distances, can be seen as a kind of 'cultural brokerage'. It is a way for tradition bearers to choose to present themselves and highlight the dynamic nature of ceremonial performances, while also refashioning the ways in which they are seen by a society that has for a large part of its history marginalised Indigenous groups. These contexts also become primary ways to keep long passed-on ceremonial traditions vibrant and relevant to the concerns of First Nations Australians today.

In recent decades the accelerated impacts of modernisation, including the introduction of new technology and other kinds of media, have also affected Warlpiri ceremonial practices – in some ways limiting prior modes of cultural transmission through fixing the forms of knowledge in videos and documentation; in other ways providing powerful new and creative means to pass on ceremonial knowledge and practices. Some examples are in the many films of ceremonial events that have been made by Yuendumu-based Pintubi Anmatjere Warlpiri (PAW) Media and Communications (previously Warlpiri Media Association) since the 1980s. Examples include the early 1980s films of the Ngajakula ceremony described in Chapter 4 and more recently *Yarripiri's Journey* (2017) recounting the Jardiwanpa (yarripiri is the Inland Taipan) Songline with ceremonial songs and embedded archival footage.[3]

HISTORY OF STAGED CEREMONIAL PERFORMANCES

The beginnings of First Nations groups performing for and with settler groups in Australia go back to the start of their first encounters. The many accounts in old newspapers and archives can reveal that there were significant public stagings of ceremonial performances in many areas across Australia. The archival film *In Song and Dance* (held at the NFSA and now available on YouTube), illustrates how Aboriginal people and groups from the region took part in a previously white-only event, the 1964 Darwin Eisteddfod.[4] This was pointedly made possible by organisers through the additions to the Eisteddfod categories of 'Corroboree' and 'Didgeridoo'. At this particular eisteddfod, groups travelled from Yirrkala, Maningrida, Tiwi Islands, Hooker Creek (now Lajamanu) and 'roughriders' from Alice Springs (as they are referred to in the film), to showcase song and dance from across a broad region of the Northern Territory. The film notes that although these groups came to Darwin to participate in these new categories, there was soon wide Aboriginal participation in other categories including choirs and solo singing performances.

The late David Gulpilil won the Darwin Australia Day Eisteddfod dance competition four times for his ceremonial dance performances. His upbringing from childhood set him up with these dance skills, which also became one of the mainstays of his acting career. Many of Gulpilil's most famous movies, including *Storm Boy*, *Walkabout*, *The Tracker*, feature ceremonial song and dance. It was at the first of these school eisteddfods that Gulpilil was spotted and cast in *Walkabout*. Through his influence on international cinema, Gulpilil was able to revolutionise the ways in which the world, including many parts of mainstream non-Indigenous Australia, saw First Nations people and culture. Unfortunately, this sometimes had the effect of perpetuating misconstrued ideas about the homogeneity of Aboriginal cultures, with Top End Yolŋu dance styles becoming known as representing the many hundreds of distinct groups across Australia. This is particularly damaging given the devastating loss of cultural heritage and ceremonial traditions resulting from early and harsh colonisation in south-eastern Australia.

Despite these issues, the opportunities in this era for a wider stage for Aboriginal ceremonial song and dance are quite remarkable given the harsh Australian Government policies under the guise of 'protection' and 'welfare' during the assimilation era (1930–1970). During that time, government policies were designed to forcibly assimilate Aboriginal people into the mainstream population. This included the banning of speaking of Indigenous languages and restricting the performance of ceremony and culture in private community and family spaces. Yorta Yorta and Dja Dja Wurrung cultural leader, visual and performance artist, curator and opera singer, Tiriki Onus, aptly describes public performance during this era as 'hiding in plain sight', referring to the ways in which Aboriginal people ensured the continued practice and performance of their culture by doing so in public, as that was the only place they were allowed to perform.[5]

Musicologist and cultural historian, Amanda Harris, in her book *Representing Australian Aboriginal Music and Dance 1930–1970*, sets out a history of Aboriginal performances in south-east Australia during this four-decade long period. She illustrates through historical accounts how Aboriginal people remained active agents in driving their own engagements and asserting their own culturally distinct modes of music and dance performance – stories that are little known despite their prominence for Australian history.[6] Aboriginal entrepreneurs led many of these events and engagements throughout this period. For example, Harris tells of the Yuin, D'harawal and Ngarigu people who represented their distinct Aboriginal cultures at the opening of the Sydney Harbour Bridge in March 1932, albeit through the required colonial framings of representation of national identity:

> The Bridge opening was marked by a massed parade in which thousands of Australians walked the length of the bridge to inaugurate the north-to-south journeys that would connect the two sides of Sydney harbour into the future. To represent this future, the pageant was led by 7,000 'young Australians'. The pageant was then designed to look backwards from this imagined future, 'depicting scenes from the history of NSW'. Leading the historical floats would be a band of Aboriginal gumleaf musicians 'dressed in war paint, with spears and boomerangs held aloft ready for a corroboree'.[7]

This book tells of many other such performances, including the 'All Aboriginal Pageant' at Wirth's Olympia, Melbourne, led by Pastor Doug Nicholls and Bill Onus, as well as 'an Aboriginal Moomba – Out of the Dark' led by Bill Onus in 1951, among many others retrieved through archival searches and enlivened through the perspectives of descendants of these trailblazing leaders.

It is this history that in numerous ways has shaped contemporary Aboriginal people's attitudes towards staged performance opportunities today, highlighting considerations around power dynamics and the role of cultural brokers, appropriate recognition through compensation, and decisions about how First Nations cultural identities will be represented. Many of these issues have emerged out of these contexts and remain central to performance opportunities that First Nations groups have today.

GLOBAL ART MOVEMENTS AND CEREMONIAL PERFORMANCE

The global recognition of Australian First Nations art has been accompanied by a rapid expansion of international appreciation for other aspects of Indigenous cultures. A broader recognition of people's identities as linked to land, kinship networks and ancestral stories has come about through artworks that feature place-based iconographic designs that link to ancestral beliefs. These artworks have been significantly shaped to be presented in ways that are aesthetically pleasing to a Western audience, and artists and the art centres can command high prices for their creative output in reciprocity for this cultural work. The audience for this artwork often has little understanding of the meaning-laden and powerful cultural symbols incorporated in them, generally only receiving brief notes of explanation with little detail about the complex ancestral stories and ways in which the works connect people to Country. Art centres are owned by a community, who employ a manager to run them, this is usually a non-Indigenous person who will interact with the market.

At a 2023 'In Conversation' event for the *Pintupi Way* exhibition of Papunya Tula art at the Drill Hall Gallery in Canberra, visiting Pintupi artists Mantua Nangala and Marlene Nampijinpa from the Kiwirrkurra community and Fred Myers, anthropologist from New York University, were asked by an audience member about Indigenous attitudes to where paintings were placed in a gallery space. Sitting with these artworks all around, Mantua, followed by Marlene, proceeded to explain the kinship relationships and broader family associations between the artists and the Country that the paintings represented. Referring to each of the paintings in the room, she spoke about the intimate connections between the artists, their families, the stories and Country of the Western Desert. In what was a hugely complex answer, Mantua and Marlene illustrated through these details how the designs central to the artwork so highly sought after internationally are deeply connected to Country and people, relationships and ancestral stories. Their response illustrating that it is certainly important to consider the way artworks are positioned in a gallery space! The exhibition *The Painters of the Wagilag Sisters Story 1937–1997*, held at the National Gallery of Australia in 1997, is a rare example of an exhibition that was culturally installed.

Intrinsic to much of this popular artwork is ceremony. Underpinning the designs are ceremonial songs, the key mode for transmitting and reproducing knowledge of Country and heritage among First Nations people. At art exhibition openings in Australian cities and internationally, artists often perform the ceremonial songs and dances that give meaning to the artwork. These important staged contexts have become contemporary ways in which First Nations people negotiate and circulate their unique identities internationally.

CEREMONIAL SONGS AND POPULAR MUSIC

My family all filed into our row of seats in the Opera House Concert Hall. We were excited to be seeing Electric Fields, performing for the first time with the Sydney Symphony Orchestra for this one night only show. It wasn't long before their energy had the audience up dancing, feeling the power of their music, the vocals in Pitjantjatjara, Yankunytjatjara and English, with the electric and orchestral grooves. The next couple of hours were filled with Zaachariaha Fielding's renowned authenticity: stories of the remote Pitjantjatjara community Mimili, of the global stage that Electric Fields had for *Eurovision*, of family and friends formed, of important First Nations history through their version of 'From Little Things, Big Things Grow', broadening knowledge of First Nations' struggles for recognition of their Land Rights and human rights. The other half of Electric Fields, keyboardist and producer Michael Ross, was equally as dazzling. Both in incredible outfits and with a strong connection to each other and to the audience.

As we left the Concert Hall, my kids singing out loud the catchy tune of 'Don't You Worry', one of Electric Fields' popular hits, my thoughts were on the last song for the evening 'Inma' – also the name of the Pitjantjatjara women's ceremonial genre that Zaachariaha had grown up with in his community of Mimili in the remote desert region of South Australia. I thought back to Zaachariaha's speech when his stunning landscape painting, also titled *Inma*, won the Wynne Prize in 2023. With senior female family from Mimili present to lead, Zaachariaha joined in to sing the ceremonial inma to accept the award.[8]

I was familiar with the Warlpiri people's deep conservatism around their ceremonial song genres, always keen for new opportunities and contexts to perform but very reluctant for these songs to be mixed with contemporary popular music genres. This is unlike the multitude of popular groups across the Top End of Australia (starting with Yothu Yindi) that do this regularly – creating new ways for these long-running traditions to be carried forward. From my encounters with Pitjantjatjara women at Law and Culture meetings, I knew that there was a similar feeling of concern about mixing these distinct musical genres – largely due to the deep respect for Ancestral Beings who are central to the songs and are the core of people's identities. Electric Fields had performed 'Inma' with profound sensitivity, beginning with a recording of Elders, then joining in softly, taking over and eventually leading the song, always leaving the vocals to dominate. The very light production was respectful of this ceremonial tradition and the culture bearers who carry it forward yet also claimed a space for it on the Opera House stage.

9

SITES OF CEREMONY

WESLEY ENOCH

I am on the southern tip of the island, walking over a sand dune and in the clearing there is a large, flattened stretch of ground with a small ridge around the edge. It is flattened from hundreds of years of dancing and gathering. The space is overgrown with grass but you can still see the distinct circle shape of the dance ground. There is something about the selection of this site as a place for ceremony – proximity to fresh water, fishing, ease of travel; there's something about the way the sunlight seems to hit the earth with an easy bounce. The soil is packed solid but also has a lightness as you walk on it, like a sprung floor in a dance studio.

I am in the inner city of Sydney at Barangaroo Reserve. There is a circle of sand laid out specifically for the dawn ceremony on 26 January. The organisers have found a flat piece of land on the slope with a view of the Harbour Bridge and the water. There is an official stand of chairs to one side for the dignitaries and the rest of the gathering perch on the hill looking down, seated in a natural amphitheatre. The temporary circle of sand is maybe 10 metres in diameter and the sand is 10 centimetres deep. A fire is smouldering away to the side and the smoke is caught by the light breeze to bathe the gathering in a healing haze. There is a speech made on a makeshift stage behind the sand circle and then the dancers come through.

I am seated out of the searing sun at the Garma Festival. The buŋgul ground is vast, with sand stretching across 30 to 50 metres or more. The crowd of 2500 is gathered right around the perimeter, so there is no front and no back to the ceremony area. From off to the side, coming from a campsite somewhere, the dance group appears. The dancers are fully decked out in yellow fabric and ochre. The songman is beside a microphone singing as they enter. They kick the sand to create fountains of yellow grit that rise high up into the air.

I am sitting in the control room of the Carrara Stadium for the Opening Ceremony of the 2018 Gold Coast Commonwealth Games. From this lofty vantage point, I can see the crowd of almost 30,000 spectators seated in a huge circle. The field, which is usually used for football games of all sorts, has been covered in sand and there is a large array of projectors creating the image of gum leaves and fire on the ground. The sand looks like it is on fire. There are 44-gallon drums dotted around the perimeter of the field, and on cue as the words are said through the headphones to those working down on the field, piles and piles of leaves are dumped on hot coals in the drums, and they spew out smoke that fills the stadium. Everyone smells the burning gum leaves.

Ceremonies happen in many different locations and can be enacted for many different reasons. From small dance grounds to large stadiums, ceremonies can happen anywhere to tell the stories of a people and create a significant moment in time. Where a ceremony occurs can indicate the relationship to the land and the story being enacted, it can also give a sense of the intended audience and what the purpose of the ceremony is. Welcoming, smoking, reinforcing Songlines, rites of passage, trade and more, there is a strong correlation between the purpose of a ceremony and where that ceremony occurs.

When I was growing up there was always a sense that there were two forms of ceremony. There was a public, outward facing set of ceremonies that could be enacted for a gathering of observers from neighbouring clans or visitors to your Country, and a second set of ceremonies that were family or inwardly focused. It was not unusual to have songs and dances, stories and art that were clearly for others to witness and observe, the retelling of stories demonstrating our connection to Country as a strong statement of reaffirmation and public evidence of cultural power and competence. Sometimes those ceremonies were playful and exuberant, perhaps a time to 'show off' the skills and dynamism of the young people and the intergenerational learning systems. They were clearly for public consumption, with amazing flourishes and consideration, and definitely a sense of there being an audience to perform for. This kind of ceremony is no less important in the cultural continuity of the clan despite the sometimes performative aspects of the delivery.

There is no hierarchy of cultural power in either the public or the private, with each needing acute observation of process and dedication to the task; the central differences revolve around who has access to the ceremony. As mentioned in an earlier chapter, cultural knowledge is not a right in the way many Western cultures express it; access to information and authority is not an innate right that people can demand. Often you have to prove your worthiness to access this information and cultural knowledge. You have to somehow demonstrate that you can handle the demands and expectations of the clan and not undermine or dilute the power of that ceremony, that you are worthy of continuing the traditions associated with the Ancestors and Elders.

It's a book being kept on a high shelf in a library. You can see it but it is out of your reach until someone can take it down for you to read, or you grow tall enough to reach it. Sometimes you can demonstrate your worthiness through dedicated observation and study only to have the book remain locked because of your gender, age, family relationships, initiation status, etc. As Georgia pointed out, for many years male anthropologists thought that only men observed ceremonies because these anthropologists were only granted access to male ceremonies. They were blinded to the powerful private female ceremonies by nature of their gender.

In 2013, I had the privilege of working with a group of amazing women who were performing sections of the Seven Sisters Songlines for the National Museum of Australia in Canberra. The women from the APY Lands wanted to help put the pieces of the Songline back together and the National Museum of Australia assisted and eventually created a large-scale performance and exhibition that celebrated the international significance of the Seven Sisters. This project looms large for both Georgia and me and indeed for this series of books on First Knowledges, and was a collaboration between the women of the Aṉangu Dancers of the APY Lands, the National Museum of Australia and the Australian National University, and powerful figures Inawintji Williamson, Diana James and Margo Ngawa Neale.

A songspiral is literally a song that navigates the landscape and may tell the story of creation. It might be shared between related communities. Songlines or songspirals are a sequence of songs that could be visualised as musical scores in which the notes in effect refer to the natural features of the land, sites of significance and their creation. Different parts of the songspiral might be shared between related communities. The drama is visibly imprinted in the land and explains its creation. This Songlines project consisted of several gatherings of relevant women mostly at sites where the Seven Sisters encountered their lustful pursuer. The women worked through the songs and dances of the Songline and then created a guided performance through the Seven Sisters story.

Part of the project included a road trip through areas of the Central Desert, revisiting the various sites to which the songs and dances referred. It was a powerful experience where the lead women would indicate the location relevant to each part of the song, and in a way I witnessed how they let the land refresh their memories and connection to place. It was as if the land was awakening the story they were singing. The women would sing and discuss the words and the songs, the dances and the body markings in an act of remembering and also to decide on the adaption for the task being undertaken. Being on Country helped connect the song and memories, helped recall the pieces and shape the story.

I was told the group of women were negotiating the memory of the storytelling and working out collectively how to tell the story for public performance. As an uninitiated man who did not speak the language I was not given access to the entirety of the story; the women handpicked their words to allow me access to certain parts of the ceremony. Some of the women's business that was occurring away from me was explained to me later, as permitted. Some parts had been passed down orally but had not been heard in decades. I could feel how ill equipped I was to understand the depth of the cultural processes being undertaken. Like the male anthropologists who crisscrossed the country for a hundred years, I got to experience just how much I didn't know.

The performance was staged outdoors, at the National Museum of Australia's amphitheatre, with large projection screens that showed images of Country and translations. During the performance, these images and text backgrounded the motion and singing of the performers. Through the repetition of song and dance, new patterns were formed and reformed for their time.

This project[1] is an example of how you may stay connected to Country with a firm sense of obligation to the past, to the memory of what has gone before while not being so rigid that this connection can't bend with changes. Rigidity is a fragility that threatens to break the very thing you are trying to preserve.

Through this project I experienced the strong sense of how ceremonies differed when they were on Country and when they were enacted off Country. I am not suggesting one was better than the other, nor am I trying to allude to one being more authentic than the other. It's more that the process of enacting ceremony on the Country is tied to had an internal focus between the dancers/singers and the land itself. While the processes I witnessed in and around Canberra were more acts of memory with a distinct purpose to express the story. This may have also been because of the nature of the project, which had a public outcome including projection, translation, theatrical lighting and amplified sound. I gained a particular insight into this difference when the ladies talked to me about some things being for 'us' and other things being for 'you'.

In the Western concept of performance there is a sense of *audience* where people observe a *performer* undertaking a practiced storytelling. This sense of performance can be seen as less ceremonial because we have distanced the notion of shared cultural values, or now see performance as a diversion or distraction from life. But even the Western sense of performance has its roots in ceremony. The Greeks thought of the actor as a conduit through which the soul of the audience member could experience the trials and tribulations of a character, to learn their lessons and feel their emotions. Brain science backs this up through identifying the mirror neuron effect, how we learn from the actions of others. This is best observed in children as they watch their parents and can mimic behaviours, language and skills. In modern times the audience–performer relationship can be seen as passive observation. Although perhaps we are underestimating the effect of seeing stories being played out and how we can file away experiences for future reference, building our emotional and narrative vocabulary to help us make sense of the world around us. Performance is ceremonial in its origins through the mimicking of animals and telling stories of hunts, creation stories and important documented moments in the history of the clan.

This sense of the audience and the performer is of great interest to me because of my work in the theatre. When I asked an Elder what the major difference was between our storytelling and the Western form of theatre, they said, 'In our ceremony there is no audience, everyone is a waiting participant who could get involved at any moment.' I translate this through the idea that everyone was an active participant in the making of First Nations ceremonies and had prior knowledge of the ceremony being enacted through long-term cultural engagement.

This is what I was witnessing as the women went through ceremony on Country. Despite my personal ignorance of the specifics of ceremony and story, I could see that the women involved were not casting the ceremony for others to observe. Every single person was actively involved, even when they were sitting out a particular dance. They would often face inward to each other, stop and converse, take breaks and repeat sections as they wished; this was not a rehearsal in the Western sense, it was an engaged exploration of the ceremony on Country. This is contrasted with the performance at the museum where there was an audience and a 'front' to perform to. Even though the ladies were doing the same dances and songs, there was a distinct sense that the people who were gathered in the 'audience' were witnessing the ceremony rather than participating in it. This did not mean the ladies were any less committed or that the ceremony was any less important, but there was a difference from being on Country that was connected to the Songline and being in Canberra where the dances and songs were a memory of that Country and place.

There has always been this distinction of focus. There is ceremony that is place based, reflecting Country and travelling through Country, and then the ceremony that is people based with the memory of Country inherent in it. Add to this the internal and external focus for 'us' and for 'you' and you get a complex relationship between land, people, purpose and time. These ideas are not mutually exclusive, and you will find overlapping and interacting intentions, a fluid sense of where the primary focus of the ceremony may be.

As part of the adaption and evolution of ceremony we have seen the development of modern ceremony into a range of locations such as theatres, corporate and tourism events, large-scale sporting events, performance and community festivals. This notion of locating ceremony for external appreciation has become an important way First Nations people have been educating the rest of the country about their history and the cultural authority of the First Australians.

It was no accident that after the 1967 referendum, communities saw arts and cultural practice as equally important to political rights, health, education, legal rights, housing and issues of incarceration. Especially in Redfern in Sydney, where we saw the growth of strong community-controlled services around these key areas, we also saw the National Black Theatre come into being. We've talked already about the political and cultural power of performance and public ceremony around events such as 26 January, the Aboriginal Tent Embassy and protests and demonstrations, but it is worth seeing how these public-facing ceremonies of storytelling also moved into theatres and auditoriums.

The Aboriginal theatre of that era expressed the plight of Aboriginal people to celebrate our survival, comment on the effects of colonialisation and educate the broader population. Gary Foley, Bob Maza, Paul Coe, Justine Saunders, Lester Bostock, Jenny Sheehan, and many others helped establish and were involved in the National Black Theatre in the 1970s. These forebears of the contemporary First Nations theatre scene in Australia had built their networks and approaches through street theatre and protests. They backed the notion that storytelling could change the hearts and minds of the population by giving insights into the history and cultural expression of Aboriginal and Torres Strait Islander peoples. In turn, this could strengthen the political struggle. The first play performed in a theatre by the National Black Theatre was Robert Merritt's *The Cake Man* in 1975, with leads Justine Saunders and Zac Martin. It tells the story of a family dealing with the colonial structures of reserves and missions. This play was revolutionary. It was a means of writing on the public record our stories and our ways. Also, it was a continuation of our cultural ceremonies and exchange of knowledge that had been occurring for millennia. The formalised relationship between audience and performers on a stage was not that different from the relationships we had seen in the large dance grounds.

In the 1970s, First Nations cultural ambition was growing. It was a time of pride and power in cultural expression. Alongside the storytelling of the theatre there was the beginnings of the Aboriginal and Islander Dance Theatre (which would go on to be NAISDA), where teachers and students balanced the current dance techniques of the world with the age-old dance traditions of this country. One of the founders of the NAISDA Dance College and Bangarra Dance Theatre was Carole Johnson, an African American dancer, choreographer and arts administrator. Carole visited Australia when she took part in the Adelaide Festival in 1972 and decided to stay. Fuelled by the civil rights movement of the United States where self-expression was equally important to Black rights and visibility, she immediately recognised the power of dance and ceremony in the push for Aboriginal and Torres Strait Islander advancement. The role of dance and story were beginning to be seen as a ceremonial expression of survival and sovereignty.

Ceremonies have helped shift public opinion when it comes to the plight of First Nations people, and over the past few decades there have been many examples of ceremony situated in theatres leading discourse and debate. The years since 1988 have been marked by the growth of significant ceremonial and cultural moments, with a formalising of cultural infrastructure, funding and personnel. Between 1988 (the 200th anniversary of the arrival of the First Fleet) and 1993 (the International Year of the World's Indigenous People) almost all the largest Indigenous arts and cultural companies in

Australia were born – some notable ones include Ilbijerri Aboriginal Torres Strait Islander Theatre Co-operative in Melbourne, Kooemba Jdarra in Brisbane, Yirra Yaakin in Perth and Bangarra Dance Theatre in Sydney. It was as if the country knew it was needing stories to be told and ceremonies to be enacted.

Ilbijerri had a breakthrough with a show called *Stolen* by Jane Harrison. The first reading of the play was in 1993 as part of Melbourne Fringe. This was a time when the story of the Stolen Generations was well known in the community but was not universally acknowledged by the Australian people. Archie Roach had released his powerful song 'Took the Children Away' in 1990, but it wasn't until the National Inquiry and the subsequent *Bringing Them Home* Report, published in 1997, that the stories of the forced removal of Aboriginal and Torres Strait Islander children from their families came into the general consciousness. *Stolen* premiered in 1998 as part of the Melbourne Festival and was immediately a sell-out success. People bought tickets to see the show almost as a way of trying to find ceremony and meaning around the devastating stories they were hearing in the media.

Stolen follows the stories of five characters through family life, removal, institutionalisation and the aftermath of life outside. In the final moments of the play the five actors drop character and talk to the audience directly of the impacts of the government policies on their lives. It is a moment where the fiction of the play is stripped away and the rawness of the ceremony of storytelling is exposed.

The show toured for years, and multiple productions have been staged. One particular moment stands out for me. In Sydney in May 2000, *Stolen* was running at the Belvoir Street Theatre, ANTAR's (Australians for Native Title and Reconciliation) Sea of Hands installation was on display, around 250,000 people walked across the Harbour Bridge, with the word 'Sorry' appearing in the sky above them, and Corroboree 2000's National Reconciliation Convention was held at the Opera House. As I noted in Chapter 6, the Convention was famous for Prime Minister John Howard expressing his 'regret' for the wrongs of the past but once again refusing to offer an apology to the Stolen Generations on behalf of the Australian Government.[2] It was also the time when Senator John Herron, Minister for Aboriginal and Torres Strait Islander Affairs, presented the Australian Government's submission to the inquiry that followed the *Bringing Them Home* Report. The submission included these statements: 'there never was a generation of stolen children' and 'the proportion of separated Aboriginal children was no more than 10 per cent'.[3]

I distinctly remember an Elder saying that 10 per cent was the literal definition of decimation. Around the same time Philip Ruddock, who in 2000 was the Federal Minister for Reconciliation, was quoted as saying that Aboriginal people had not invented the wheel and had no experience of advanced civilisation[4] – as a comment on our disadvantage.

Within three days of these events the play had sold out again. People flocked to be in the audience to help understand the emotional and political landscape they were experiencing.

My analysis is that we need ceremony to process the events of the world, however the ceremony might be presented. People can read the newspapers and understand the intellectual and philosophical ideas, but they need ceremony to ground these thoughts, to provide powerful anchors in the spiritual and cultural. As human beings we crave collective moments of storytelling and to find a way we can fit in. Ceremonies in every form help shape the way we see ourselves and our communities and gives us a vocabulary to understand the past and shape the future.

The Sydney Olympic Opening Ceremony in 2000, watched by 3.7 billion people, was not only a celebration of Australianness, it was a time to reinforce our connection to our long history. These large sporting events are a time for a country to showcase their athletes, sporting culture and their national narratives. It is a time to talk to the world about who you are and the aspirations of the country. Stephen Page, who had been in charge at Bangarra Dance Theatre since 1991, was given the responsibility to create an Indigenous component to the Opening Ceremony. The ceremonial aspects of an Olympic or Commonwealth Games Opening Ceremony or any major sporting event often includes flag raising, processions of the athletes, lighting of flames and relays, official speeches, and the like. These ceremonies are a time to instil pride and power, especially important in this era of mixed signals and questioning. The chance to hear Aboriginal languages, to see hundreds of Aboriginal dancers from all over the country in full paint up, the urban young people in metallic materials, the demonstration of men's and women's business, the smoking ceremony, the stilt walking Mimi spirits and the raising of the Wandjina image created an amazing feeling. Playing the video footage again now, you can hear the audience reaction at the simple gesture of putting Aboriginal and Torres Strait Islander people centre stage of an 80,000-seat stadium as well as a global viewing audience that was almost two-thirds of the world's population at the time.

There have been other Opening Ceremonies in Australia since the 2000 Olympics. In 2006 at the Commonwealth Games in Melbourne there was a great deal of conversation about making space for First Nations people inside and outside the stadium and that the cultural legacy should live beyond the seven minutes of the Indigenous Section titled 'My Skin, My Life'. Many of us involved in the Opening Ceremony were also advocates to the Games organisers to facilitate a camp site in the Fitzroy Gardens, East Melbourne, where a campfire/sacred fire was lit to host debate and discussion around First Nations issues and cultural responses to the colonial project the Games represented. Inside the stadium we were celebrating the cultural significance of reawakening the practice of making possum skin cloaks to represent story and Country, issuing a song welcome through conversations with Elders to offer Wominjeka, which roughly translates as 'To come with purpose' and is commonly used as a welcome. The cloaks were created by a group of amazing artists including Vicki Couzens, Maree Clarke, Lee Darroch and Treahna Hamm, with Elders from across the Victoria clans. Using records and artefacts, these artists designed and made the cloaks with an express purpose to be used in their communities for ceremonies such as births, deaths, when officiating over marriages and to help encourage greater cultural purpose. Almost as a side note to making these cloaks and their designs depicting Country, they were displayed as part of the Opening Ceremony as a sign of cultural authority and power. The ceremony inside the stadium witnessed by the many and the ceremonies outside the stadium almost mirror the internal and external purpose of ceremonies for time immemorial. The notion of 'us' and 'you'.

In 2018, when I was involved in devising the Opening Ceremony of the Gold Coast Commonwealth Games, we had an interesting debate about when the smoking and Welcome to Country should occur. In recent times, the idea is that a Welcome should be given at the very beginning of the event, but Elders mentioned that the real welcome had to happen once the athletes had arrived as they were the people who most needed the care of the spirits. So there was an Acknowledgement of Country at the start of the ceremony for all in the stadium and those viewing on their screens, and a fuller Welcome to Country once all the athletes had paraded onto the field. Also, we discussed how to smoke a massive stadium of people when it is often done on a small and intimate scale. One response to this was that a senior person was selected to smoke the visiting dignitaries in the royal box. Scale and purpose dictated the form and execution of these cultural ceremonies while not affecting the purpose.

Throughout this book we have often written about the dynamic nature of First Nations cultures and that they are not trapped in an old museum-style feedback loop of extinction or unresponsiveness to the modern world. Where these ceremonies occur may change and comment on the modernity of First Nations people, but their core stays the same. Whether on Country, dance grounds covered with sand, elevated stages or large stadiums; whether performed as intimate family-based, repeated rituals or large-scale events viewed by billions, there is no hierarchy of legitimacy. There are processes and traditions that must be adhered to, to maintain the cultural integrity of the ceremony.

10

CEREMONIES FOR THE FUTURE

GEORGIA CURRAN

It was April 2024, and I was once more camped with my Warlpiri friends and families – our swags grouped around small campfires across a section of an expansive sandy creek bed. It had rained recently, and we could feel the cold water was only a few metres beneath us. The air was fresh and the Country felt healthy. *Minyiranyira minyiranyira*, I sung in my head and breathed in deeply. My 'sister' and lead for women's business in Yuendumu, Lorraine Nungarrayi Granites, smiled at me, almost like she knew what I was feeling. I had learned this word that's used in many Warlpiri songs from Nungarrayi and my other elderly Warlpiri companions. It refers to the way the Country smells after rain, when it is clean, and its rich essence is strong in the air.

Minyirainyira x 2	The smell of the wet earth
Walarajarra x 2	The digging sticks (the ancestral women)
Kanalyurrparna x 2	I am in one group

A:	mi	nyi	ra	nyi	ra
B:	wa	la	ra	jar	ra
C:	ka	na	lyurr	pa	rna

A: Minyiranyira (The smell of the wet earth)
B: Walarajarra (The women's digging sticks)
C: Kanalyurrpa-rna (I am in one big group)

A rhythm and text of a verse from Warlpiri women's Minamina yawulyu 'travelling women's ceremonies'.

Nungarrayi and I quietly hummed this verse, one of many from the Minamina 'travelling women' yawulyu, which Warlpiri women sing frequently.[1] In a way typical of Warlpiri songs, one word connotes so much – a rich infusion of ancestral spirit evoked by the word 'minyiranyira', in the smell of Country, but also in the oil and ochre on bodies, within objects like the kuturu ceremonial poles, and in headdresses, feathers and necklaces that are used for ceremonies. This deep essence of ancestral spirit is in the tune of a song. It is in the dancers' bodies as they experience the collective high of a sort that you know is good for your spirit and your soul.

By early evening my chest was shining with red and white ochred designs and oil. I'd been painted with the Ngarlu 'honey flower' designs – belonging to Ruth Napaljarri Oldfield, my pimirdi, my aunty, who with her sisters had given me my skin name, Nungarrayi, when I first arrived to live in Yuendumu many years earlier. This was clearly a strategic move; she had placed me in a social role so that she could share with me, and I could support her to write down and record the deep knowledge of her ceremonial song traditions, which she had inherited from her father. Today my social placing in a Warlpiri world is so much a part of who I am. When the painted design had been finished, I went over to Ruth who inspected my chest and arms closely before asserting, 'Ngurrju-nyayirni' ('really good'). She broke into a proud smile. She was getting very old and hadn't been able to dance now for many years. I felt good representing Ngarlu for her, for her deceased sisters, for us all.

Southern Ngaliya Warlpiri women worry that girls do not have the opportunity to learn their ceremonial traditions in the same way that they used to when they were young. Unlike when the current generation of senior women were growing up, there are no longer women's ceremonies held frequently as a part of everyday life. Due to this concern, they have created this new ceremonial tradition. As I wrote about earlier, each April and September, a large group of women gather at a different remote outstation, away from community life and pressures, and on Country. They have organised external support from Incite Arts, funded through their own royalty monies, to ensure everything that is needed to make this work – food, transport, bedding – is taken care of. The Southern Ngaliya dance camps have all the elements of a good ceremony – repetition, lots of kids, Elders, young women, stories, songs, dances and painted designs that link Warlpiri women to who they are today and where they come from. Deep links to the past, to the Jukurrpa Ancestors who create the world, are seen in ceremonies held now.

These Southern Ngaliya dance camps, like all ceremonies for today, shape the way the world is and provide a context to renegotiate everything that is important. It isn't always easy to get all the women in one place at the right time given people's complex lives with family, work and the inevitable demands of community life. But the dance camps are prioritised because, as Warlpiri women recognise, the wellbeing of their grandchildren depends on ensuring that ceremony keeps going.

This book sets forth the clear importance of ceremony across time and place for First Nations people around Australia. We have outlined many of the contexts in which ceremonies are held today. Welcomes to Country, smoking ceremonies, rites of passages, festivals, staged performances, or grand, large-scale events, are all contemporary ways in which current generations link deeply to their past and to a cultural identity fundamental to wellbeing. The continuation of these ceremonies is important cultural work, for communities and on a national level to recognise and celebrate Australia's First Nations' history and culture. This notion of continuity has been emphasised often in this book and in the First Knowledges series.

But what kind of ceremonies form part of this future? Australia's brutal colonial history has had an enormous impact on the continuity of ceremonial traditions in many parts of the country. This history has prevented access to and continuation of the practice of ceremonies fundamental to precolonial First Nations worlds. Reclaiming ceremonies today is vital to reform these continuities with the past and move towards the future. Some of the examples in this book illustrate how ceremonies can be revived from archival sources, by consultations with Elders and through creative adaptation and borrowing from neighbouring groups.

I often think of the Wangkumara people who I worked with in Bourke, New South Wales. Of their stories and songs that we heard together on recordings, from the clever Old People who had engaged in recording efforts, foreseeing and having already experienced so much disruption. They made sure that there would be a way for these ceremonial songs to be accessed again in the future. I think of all the different mobs across Australia, who work hard to revive these ceremonial practices through accessing archives, creative adaption and deep commitment to providing contexts in which to hold these ceremonies. I think of my Wangaaypuwan/Ngiyampaa/Wiradjuri colleague Jesse Hodgetts, who told me that the types of Warlpiri songs set out by senior Warlpiri man Thomas Jangala Rice, in which he described place-based, travelling and ceremonially functional songs, had felt familiar for his mob and resonated in a way that helped to make sense of their own ceremonial categories.[2] Reclaiming these ceremonial songs by these incredible First Nations culture bearers, through deep engagement with their pasts and the efforts of their Old People, puts the focus on what is most important – performing these ceremonies today, right now.

On a warm Friday evening in November 2024, I was in Fremantle after a hectic week at a conference in Perth. Detracting from the busy-ness of the growing Friday night crowd, the sun overruled with its soft dominance in a way it only does on Nyoongar Boodja. Clint Bracknell, Wirlomin Nyoongar musician and researcher, was scheduled to present a public lecture at an intimate event at the Kidogo Arthouse on the main beach – his wife's Country. Clint is known for his incredible Nyoongar song revitalisation projects, including the Nyoongar Wonderland and Song Circle of recent years. That evening he spoke of how a few years earlier one of his Elders had come to him asking why they sing the same songs all the time, when there are so many more in Country that they should also be singing. Clint referenced the late Warlpiri Elder, Rex Japanangka Granites, who assured through his words 'that Country never changes', honouring how Country holds ceremonial songs forever so they are there to be accessed when needed by the people who share their same ancestral spirit.[3] So accompanied by Elders, he went on to spend slow time, deep listening in Country so they could take care to receive these songs. And, as Clint told us, it wasn't long before the songs came to them. In a real treat for the audience at this event, Clint led the singing, joined by his wife, both with clapsticks keeping a strong beat with two adult dancers and also his young son. These songs had a distinct Nyoongar sound, learned from the Old People, from archival recordings and from attentive listening in Country. The vitality of these ceremonial songs was clear.[4] There are many ways to carry ceremony into the future.

WESLEY ENOCH

THE CEREMONY OF TRUTH-TELLING

I'm sitting in the local hall on the island, surrounded by my Elders and community. This is the same hall where my father's funeral was held almost ten years earlier, the place we gathered before walking 1 kilometre to the cemetery. I have a photo of myself outside this hall at the age of nine dressed in a brown vinyl jacket when my family attended a wedding there in 1978. This is the same hall where decades of funerals, weddings, community meetings and parties have been held, there are weird, neglected pieces of sticky tape and string on the walls, memories of where decorations were once attached. My father had his sixtieth birthday here a few years before he died, a fantastic gathering of families and friends, speeches and photos. Today it is a gathering of a different type.

There is dancing outside the hall, a welcoming ceremony and a smoking. A cleansing before we enter this space. This hall has been here long before this moment in time. The old Benevolent Asylum built it back in 1913 as a men's mess hall but now the community owns it; well, we don't own it in the whitefellas' eyes but we do really due to the years of ceremony here. If you have the stories of a place, you have ownership over it, and it has ownership over you. The tears and grief in the floorboards, the joys and triumphs in the memories of the nails and the songs and prayers in the roof beams have rewritten the origin story of this building and replaced it with ceremonies of us, of our community.

Today is a week on from a state election where the new government came to power promising to stop the truth-telling process, which had started years earlier through multiple conversations about the need for change. In this very hall there were gatherings to talk about recognition in the Constitution and the movement that became the Uluru Statement from the Heart asking for Voice, Treaty, Truth and a Makarrata Commission. The new state government had campaigned in the lead-up to the election that they would stop this process that had been going for decades, and true to their word they did.

We are gathered here today to start a formal process of truth-telling, even if the Queensland Government doesn't want it. We don't need permission to start something that has been going on for years. We don't need governments to tell us we can't gather and talk together – black and white, those from here and those who have come from other places. There is a television camera up the back of the room ready to film it, as this may be the first truth-telling session to occur since the newly elected government halted the process and froze the funding. Various Elders stand and speak of our community, our clans, our struggles, our histories. The room is full of eager ears and receptive hearts. There are tears. There are some chuckles. There is a reverent hush. There is definitely a sense for all those gathered here that we are in ceremony.

After the Voice referendum there was a real sense of *Where do we go from here?* If we were going to be denied a formally recognised Voice in the Constitution then *What was the next step?* Because we aren't going to go away. Our history is not going to magically disappear because others don't want to deal with how our yesterdays have brought us here to our today. Truth-telling is the next step. Maybe it was always the way forward. Maybe it is truly the missing step.

On the island you can still see YES signs in people's front yards. There is a graffiti YES spray painted on a sign on the main drag. You can still feel the disappointment, the sense that history is repeating, and we must tell our stories again and again and again. That is alright, we are built for it. We know how to tell our story. In the aftermath of the referendum there was so much soul searching and hurt, blame and finger pointing, and I was not immune to it. Immediately after the referendum result Elders across the country asked for a time of silence and reflection, a ceremony to stop and think about the outcome and what it might mean. A ceremony of silence. Like when we take a minute's silence on ANZAC Day, but such was the sense of loss that only a week could provide the appropriate ceremony.

This made me reflect on those kids in detention I had worked with back in the 1990s (where are they now?) and the people who had established the Day of Mourning in 1938 (how their struggle had informed the past century of Indigenous Policy). I thought about the ladies of the Seven Sisters Project and how they were keeping stories alive, wondered what they felt about this sense of rejection. All the storytellers who had written the plays, the protestors, the filmmakers and the dancers. This country moves forward when we embrace ceremony, when it celebrates the process of remaking all that we have learnt from the past to find new ways of our history being alive today.

Maybe this country needs more ceremony to come to terms with who we are and what we have done to be where we are, here and now. Maybe we need less politics, less campaigning where values and morals are traded for money and power.

I reflect on the Voice to Parliament Yes campaign and think, *What could I have done differently?* How could I have helped create more ceremony in this country to bring people through a rite of passage and become something new in the eyes of the global community, to grow, to learn? What forms of diplomacy are missing? What business needs to be done before we can change? Hindsight is a dangerous viewpoint but maybe we needed more ceremony throughout the campaign.

Back at the hall, my aunty says, 'Ceremony activates the life force of the land, taking us back to connect with our Ancestors. The blood spilt has never been healed. We need a healing ceremony for Mother Earth, us – her children – and all her adopted children.'

She talks about a lake that is a window that pierces the outer crust of this sand island and you can see deep into the aquifer, deep down into the heart of the fresh water. She talks about the ceremonies that would happen around this lake and how they connect us to the thousands of generations who have lived in this place. By looking into that lake, you can look back in time to when time began. She says, 'It is those who fear the truth who attempt to hinder it,' and she is right.

I know the only way forward is to find more ceremony for truth-telling, making safe, welcoming spaces that do not perpetuate guilt or bitterness, not where we the children of this land tell our story again and again talking of our trauma and our pain, but where all the 'adopted' children find ways of accessing the power of our history. Where all Australians embrace all the yesterdays. In years from now I hope we can look back and see this as a time of transition. From only seeing the disappointment and sorrow of the past to a powerful sense of tomorrow remade from our past.

ULURU STATEMENT FROM THE HEART

We, gathered at the 2017 National Constitutional Convention, coming from all points of the southern sky, make this statement from the heart:

Our Aboriginal and Torres Strait Islander tribes were the first sovereign Nations of the Australian continent and its adjacent islands, and possessed it under our own laws and customs. This our ancestors did, according to the reckoning of our culture, from the Creation, according to the common law from 'time immemorial', and according to science more than 60,000 years ago.

This sovereignty is *a spiritual notion: the ancestral tie between the land, or 'mother nature', and the Aboriginal and Torres Strait Islander peoples who were born therefrom, remain attached thereto, and must one day return thither to be united with our ancestors. This link is the basis of the ownership of the soil, or better, of sovereignty.* It has never been ceded or extinguished, and co-exists with the sovereignty of the Crown.

How could it be otherwise? That peoples possessed a land for sixty millennia and this sacred link disappears from world history in merely the last two hundred years?

With substantive constitutional change and structural reform, we believe this ancient sovereignty can shine through as a fuller expression of Australia's nationhood.

Proportionally, we are the most incarcerated people on the planet. We are not an innately criminal people. Our children are aliened from their families at unprecedented rates. This cannot be because we have no love for them. And our youth languish in detention in obscene numbers. They should be our hope for the future.

These dimensions of our crisis tell plainly the structural nature of our problem. This is *the torment of our powerlessness.*

We seek constitutional reforms to empower our people and take *a rightful place* in our own country. When we have power over our destiny our children will flourish. They will walk in two worlds and their culture will be a gift to their country.

We call for the establishment of a First Nations Voice enshrined in the Constitution.

Makarrata is the culmination of our agenda: *the coming together after a struggle.* It captures our aspirations for a fair and truthful relationship with the people of Australia and a better future for our children based on justice and self-determination.

We seek a Makarrata Commission to supervise a process of agreement-making between governments and First Nations and truth-telling about our history.

In 1967 we were counted, in 2017 we seek to be heard. We leave base camp and start our trek across this vast country. We invite you to walk with us in a movement of the Australian people for a better future.

ACKNOWLEDGEMENTS

My contributions to this book come from a variety of lived experiences and conversations over a career. There are so many people to thank who have shaped my thinking and approach to Ceremony – Uncle Frank, Uncle Norman, Uncle Brian and Uncle Will, Maureen Watson, Aunty Kath (Oodgeroo Noonuccal), Michael and Ludmilla Doneman, Lafe Charlton, Nunka Raymond Walker, Stephen Page, Lydia Miller, Deborah Mailman, Hilary Beaton, Wendy Blacklock, Jacob Nash, Lily Shearer, Liza-Mare Syron, and the many First Nations artists who work to tell stories and make Ceremony.

I extend my deepest thanks to the Garma Festival and the Yothu Yindi Foundation for their ongoing cultural leadership and inspiration. My gratitude also goes to the Annamila First Nations Foundation for their tireless commitment to strengthening First Nations voices and futures. I acknowledge the Minjerribah and Moorgumpin Elders in Council, whose wisdom and guidance continue to shape my understanding of Country, culture and community – in particular, Aunty Maureen, Aunty Mary and Dale, Aunty Evie and Uncle Alan, and Delvene.

I offer thanks to my creative collaborators from the 2006 Commonwealth Games in Melbourne and the 2018 Commonwealth Games on the Gold Coast – your shared vision and dedication helped bring bold cultural statements to life on the world stage. My appreciation also goes to the National Museum of Australia and the extraordinary team behind *Kungkarangkalpa: Seven Sisters Songline*, especially Sally Scales, Inawintji Williamson,

Margo Ngawa Neale, Helen Healy, and Robin Archer from the Centenary of Canberra 2013 – thank you for your stewardship of stories and connection. Noel Pearson, *The Saturday Paper*, Corey Zerna and Jess Moran, Creative Australia and Queensland University of Technology.

To my family, who ground me and give me my history, and to my partner David, whose support allows me to soar.

To my dad who left us too early, but even in death teaches me humility and connection. –WE

My biggest thanks go to the Warlpiri individuals and families who have generously shared their world with me, especially Coral Napangardi Gallagher,* Ruth Napaljarri Oldfield, Judy Nampijinpa Granites,* Lorraine Nungarrayi Granites, Lynette Nampijinpa Granites, Maisie Napurrurla Wayne, Nellie Nangala Wayne, Bessie Nakamarra Sims,* Alice Nampijinpa Henwood, Lee Nangala Wayne, Peggy Nampijinpa Brown, Katrina Nampijinpa Brown, Maggie Napaljarri Ross,* Jean Napanangka Brown, Margaret Napanangka Brown, Enid Nangala Gallagher, Ormay Nangala Gallagher, Yvonne Nangala Gallagher, Marlette Napurrurla Ross, Louanna Napangardi Williams, Barbara Napanangka Martin, Nancy Napurrurla Oldfield, Nancy Nungarrayi Collins, Cecily Napanangka Granites, Reilly Jupurrurla Oldfield,* Otto Jungarrayi Sims,* Wendy Nungarrayi Sims, Lynn Nungarrayi Sims, Valerie Napaljarri Martin, Simon Japangardi Fisher Snr., Thomas Jangala Rice, Jeannie Nungarrayi Egan,* Harry Jakamarra Nelson* and Rex Japanangka Granites.* I extend this gratitude to all the other

* Denotes that the person has passed away.

yawulyu-wardingki ladies and ceremony men of Southern Ngaliya Country, as well as culture bearers from across Australia.

I also acknowledge my academic colleagues whose discussions over many years have helped to shape my understanding of ceremony and the ways I have presented my understanding in this book. Particular thanks to Nicolas Peterson and Laura Case for their generosity in providing comments on this manuscript, but also to Mary Laughren, Yasmine Musharbash, Françoise Dussart, Stephen Wild, Linda Barwick, Myfany Turpin, Fred Myers, Richard Moyle, Clint Bracknell, Reuben Brown, Evelyn Quispe, Amanda Harris, Payi Linda Ford, Jesse Hodgetts, Catherine Ingram, Mahesh White-Radhakrishnan, Toby Martin, and James Humberstone.

My thanks must also be extended to my family for always being a part of the journey. –GC

IMAGE CREDITS

Front inside cover	Warlpiri women dance the Pamapardu yawulyu 'flying termite women's ceremonies' for a Southern Ngaliya dance camp at Old Nyirrpi. Pictured: Lee Nangala Wayne (front) and Enid Nangala Gallagher (behind) Image Credit: Incite Arts.
Back inside cover	Aboriginal Australian electronic music duo Electric Fields performing onstage. Pictured: Zaachariaha Fielding and Michael Ross Image credit: Mushroom Creative House.
28	Spiral illustration based on original illustration by Wesley Enoch.
40	'Corroboree' by Tommy McRae. From the book of drawing by Tommy McRae and Mickey of Ulladulla, approximately 1860-1901 Pen & ink, 23.3 × 33.8 cm Sourced from Mitchell Library, State Library of New South Wales.
44	Warlpiri women painting up with Mala kuruwarri 'Rufous Hare Wallaby Dreaming designs' from Jila (Chilla Well). Pictured: Nancy Nungarrayi Collins (being painted), (left–right) Maisie Napurrurla Wayne, Peggy Nampijinpa Brown, Alice Nampijinpa Michaels and Marlette Napurrurla Ross. Image Credit: Incite Arts.

108 Section of Aboriginal meeting in Australian Hall, Sydney, organised by Aborigines' Progressive Association mourners
Aborigines day of mourning, 26 January 1938
Published in *Man Magazine*, Mar–Apr, 1938, Sydney, NSW
Photo: Russell Clark
Sourced from Mitchell Library, State Library of New South Wales.

167 A rhythm and text of a verse from Warlpiri women's Minamina yawulyu 'travelling women's ceremonies'. Originally published: Warlpiri Women from Yuendumu. 2017. *Yurntumu-wardingki juju-ngaliya-kurlangu yawulyu*: Warlpiri women's songs from Yuendumu. Batchelor Institute Press (Chapter 1, p. 18).

NOTES

1. PERSONAL PERSPECTIVES

1 Ainslie Roberts with text by Charles P. Mountford, *The Dreamtime: Australian Aboriginal Myths in Paintings*, Rigby, Adelaide, 1970.

2 Georgia Curran, *Sustaining Indigenous Songs: Contemporary Warlpiri Ceremonial Life in Central Australia*, Berghahn, New York, 2020.

3 See Peggy Nampijinpa Brown telling the Warlukurlangu story and Warlpiri women dancing the Warlukurlangu yawulyu, at: <https://ictv.com.au/video/item/4989>.

2. WHAT IS CEREMONY?

1 M Neale & L Kelly, *Songlines: The Power and Promise*, Thames & Hudson, Melbourne, 2020, Chapter 9.

2 Phyllis Kaberry, *Aboriginal Woman Sacred and Profane*, Routledge, UK,1939.

3 M Neale & L Kelly, *Songlines*, Thames & Hudson, Melbourne, 2020.

4 Stan Grant, 'A World Divided', Keynote, Integrity 20'18 Launch, Griffith University, 2018, <https://integrity20.org/media/stan-grant-keynote/>.

5 Myfany Turpin, Felicity Meakins, Brenda Croft, *Songs from the Stations: Wajarra as performed by Ronnie Wavehill Wirrpnga, Topsy Dodd Ngarnjal and Dandy Danbayarri at Kalkaringi*, Sydney University Press, NSW, 2019.

6 Arnold Van Gennep, *The Rites of Passage*, University of Chicago Press, Chicago, 1960.

7 Georgia Curran, *Sustaining Indigenous Songs: Contemporary Warlpiri Ceremonial Life in Central Australia*, Berghahn, New York, 2020.

8 Jakelin Troy, Linda Barwick, 'Claiming the "Song of the Women of the Menero Tribe"', *Musicology Australia*, 42(2), 2021, pp 85–107.

9 Maya Haviland, Wayne Barker (Producers), *Following the Trade Routes: Exchanges and innovations in cultural economy*, Kimberley Aboriginal Law and Culture Centre and Australian National University, 2022.

10 Myfany Turpin, Calista Yeoh & Clint Bracknell, 'Wanji-wanji: The past and future of an Aboriginal travelling song', *Musicology Australia*, 42(2), 2020, pp 123–47.

11 Stephen Wild, 'Rom in Canberra', *Australian Aboriginal Studies*, 1, 1983, pp 55–59.

12 Rachael Knowles, 'How this Makassan man came to dance with Gumatj at Garma', National Indigenous Television (NITV), 14 August 2023, <www.sbs.com.au/nitv/article/how-this-makassan-man-came-to-dance-with-gumatj-at-garma/qkq2pf9aj>.

13 Rolf de Heer, Peter Djigirr (Directors), *Ten Canoes*, Palace Films and Cinemas, 2006.

14 M Langton & A Corn, *Law: The Way of the Ancestors*, Thames & Hudson, Melbourne, 2023, Chapter 5.

4. WORLDS OF RELATIONSHIPS – WARLPIRI CEREMONIES HELD TODAY

1 For a fuller description of the songs and dance styles for Kurdiji see Georgia Curran, *Sustaining Indigenous Songs*, Berghahn, New York, 2020.

2 Mervyn Meggitt, 'Initiation among the Warlpiri' in *Religion in Aboriginal Australia: An anthology*, edited by Max Charlesworth, Howard Morphy, Diane Bell & Kenneth Maddock, University of Queensland Press, Qld, pp 285–98, 1984. Stephen Wild, 'Walbiri Music and Dance in their Social and Cultural Nexus', PhD thesis. Indiana University, Department of Anthropology, Bloomington, 1975.

3 Fred R Myers, *Pintupi Country, Pintupi Self*, University of California Press, Berkeley, 1991.Georgia Curran, *Sustaining Indigenous Songs*, Berghahn, New York 2020.
4 For a fuller account of a Warawata ceremony held in 2007, see Georgia Curran, *Sustaining Indigenous Songs*, Berghahn, New York, 2020.
5 Nicolas Peterson, 'An Expanding Domain: Mobility and the Initiation Journey', *Oceania*, 70(3), 2000, pp 205–18.
6 Ned Lander, Rachel Perkins (Producers), *Jardiwarnpa: A Warlpiri Fire Ceremony* (videorecording), Blood Brothers series, Part 1, Australian Film Finance Corporation, City Pictures, Sydney, 1993.
7 Georgia Curran, '"Waiting for Jardiwanpa": History and Mediation in Warlpiri Fire Ceremonies', *Oceania*, 89(1), 2019, pp 20–35.
8 Coral Napangardi Gallagher & Peggy Nampijinpa Brown with Georgia Curran and Barbara Napanangka Martin, *Jardiwanpa yawulyu: Warlpiri women's songs from Yuendumu* (book with CD), Batchelor Institute Press, Batchelor, NT, 2014.
9 Nicolas Peterson, 'Buluwandi: A Central Australia ceremony for the resolution of conflict', in *Australian Aboriginal Anthropology: Modern Studies in the Social Anthropology of the Australian Aborigines*, edited by RM Berndt, University of Western Australia Press, Nedlands, WA, 1970, pp 200–15. Petronella Vaarzon-Morel, George Jungarrayi Ryder, Teddy Jupurrurla Long, Jim Wafer & Luke Kelly, 'Reanimating Ngajakula: Lander Warlpiri songs of connection and transformation', in *Vitality and Change in Warlpiri Songs*, edited by Georgia Curran, Linda Barwick, Valerie Napaljarri Martin, Simon Japangardi Fisher & Nicolas Peterson, Sydney University Press/ Pintubi Anmatjer Warlpiri Media and Communications, Sydney and Yuendumu, 2024, pp 257–83.

10 Curran, Georgia & Françoise Dussart, '"We don't show our women's breasts for nothing": Shifting purposes for Warlpiri women's public rituals – yawulyu – Central Australia, 1980s–2020s', *Studies in Religion/ Sciences Religieuses*, 52(4), 2023, pp 601–18.

5. ADAPTION AND EVOLUTION

1 'Garma 2009: Investiture Awards Order of Australia to Local Leaders at Garma Festival', Yothu Yindi Foundation, YouTube video and transcript, 2009, </www.youtube.com/watch?v=vmIk5c4Ga4o>.

2 Stanner coined the term 'everywhen' in his 1956 essay 'The Dreaming'; see: '*The Dreaming' & Other Essays*, Black Inc. Agenda, Melbourne, 2009.

3 See: 'The "Bombing of Darwin" Dance by Tiwi Mob', ICTV Play, filmed in 1987, <https://ictv.com.au/video/item/11717>. 'Tiwi islanders dance in remembrance of Indigenous war effort – video', *Guardian Australia*, 14 October 2015, <www.theguardian.com/australia-news/video/2015/oct/14/tiwi-men-women-dance-darwin-bombing-remembrance-indigenous-war-effort-video>.

6. CEREMONY AS A POLITICAL ACT

1 See: National Museum of Australia, '1938: Sesquicentenary and Aboriginal Day of Mourning', <www.nma.gov.au/defining-moments/resources/day-of-mourning>.

2 See: *NAIDOC history*, <www.naidoc.org.au/about/history>.

3 Noel Pearson, 'Declaration of Australia: three epic strands in a grand narrative', Cape York Partnership, 16 September 2017, <https://capeyorkpartnership.org.au/declaration-of-australia-three-epic-strands-in-a-grand-narrative-noel-pearson/>.

7. INTERREGIONAL FESTIVALS

1 M Meggitt, *The Gadjari among the Walbiri Aborigines of Central Australia*, Oceania Monographs: no. 14, University of Sydney, 1966.

2 M Meggitt, 1966, p. 194.

3 M Meggitt, 1966, p. 197.

4 Ronald Berndt, *Kunapipi: A Study of an Australian Aboriginal Religious Cult*. FW Cheshire, Melbourne, 1951.

5 Kim McKenzie, *Waiting for Harry*, AIAS Film Unit Production, 1980.

6 Stephen Wild, 'Walbiri Music and Dance in Their Social and Cultural Nexus', PhD thesis, Indiana University, 1975.

7 See The Laura Quinkan Dance Festival site: < www.lauraquinkanfestival.com.au/pages/about/>.

8 See Barunga Festival site: <https://barungafestival.com.au/about/>.

8. STAGING CEREMONY

1 See Georgia Curran, 'Incorporating archival cultural heritage materials into contemporary Warlpiri women's yawulyu spaces', in Linda Barwick, Jennifer Green & Petronella Vaarzon-Morel (eds), *Archival Returns: Central Australia and Beyond*, Sydney University Press, Sydney, 2020, pp 91–110. Georgia Curran & Françoise Dussart, '"We don't show our women's breasts for nothing": Shifting purposes for Warlpiri women's public rituals – yawulyu – Central Australia, 1980s–2020s', *Studies in Religion – Science Religieuses*, 52(4), 2023. Georgia Curran & Enid Nangala Gallagher, 'Yawulyu mardu-kuja-patu-kurlangu: Relational Dynamics of Warlpiri Women's Song Performance', *Journal of Intercultural Studies* 44(5): 716–33, 2023.

2 See Georgia Curran & Otto Jungarrayi Sims, 'Performing purlapa: Projecting Warlpiri Identity in a Globalised World', *The Asia Pacific Journal of Anthropology*, 22 (2–3), 2021, pp 203–19.

3 See Roger Sandall & Nicolas Peterson, 'A Warlbiri fire ceremony, Ngatjakula' (motion picture), Australian Institute of Aboriginal Studies, Canberra, 1977 (1967). Simon Japanangka Fisher Jnr & Jason Japaljarri Woods, *Songlines – Yarripiri's Journey*, 'Songlines on Screen', National Indigenous Television/Screen Australia, 2018.

4 *In song and dance*, directed by Lee Robinson, edited by Don Saunders, produced by Joy Cavill, Australian Commonwealth Film Unit/ Waratah Film Productions, ACMI, 1964.

5 Amanda Harris, *Representing Australian Aboriginal Music and Dance 1930–1970*, Bloomsbury, London, 2020.

6 Amanda Harris, 2020.

7 Amanda Harris, pp 28–29, 2020.

8 Art Gallery NSW website, 'Winner: Wynne Prize 2023, Zaachariaha Fielding, *Inma*', <www.artgallery.nsw.gov.au/prizes/wynne/2023/30577/>.

9. SITES OF CEREMONY

1 Kungkarangkalpa: Seven Sisters Songline, <www.youtube.com/watch?v=3igXR7oL8FU>.

2 National Museum of Australia, 'Defining Moments: Walk for Reconciliation', <www.nma.gov.au/defining-moments/resources/walk-for-reconciliation>.

3 Human Rights and Equal Opportunity Commission, 'Us Taken-Away Kids: Commemorating the 10th anniversary of the Bringing Them Home Report' p. 19.

4 *Washington Post*, 4 July 2000, see: <https://www.greenleft.org.au/content/world-according-ruddock>.

10. CEREMONIES FOR THE FUTURE

1 Warlpiri Women from Yuendumu (edited by Georgia Curran), *Yurntumu-wardingki juju-ngaliya-kurlangu yawulyu: Warlpiri women's songs from Yuendumu* (inc. DVD), Batchelor Institute Press, Batchelor, NT, 2017.
2 Jesse Hodgetts, 'A Review of Indigenous Song Publications to Guide and Think About Language and Song Revitalisation in New South Wales', *Musicology Australia*, 2025.
3 Georgia Curran, Linda Barwick, Valerie Napaljarri Martin, Simon Japangardi Fisher & Nicolas Peterson, *Vitality and Change in Warlpiri Songs*, Sydney University Press/PAW Media and Communications, Sydney/Yuendumu, 2024.
4 Clint Bracknell, *Maatakitj* (self-titled), recorded/rendered creative work, 2023.

FURTHER RESOURCES

BOOKS

Bracknell, Clint, *Natj Waalanginy (What Singing?): Nyungar song from the South-West of Western Australia*, PhD thesis, University of Western Australia, 2016.

Brown, Reuben, *The Gift of Song: Performing Exchange in Western Arnhem Land*, Routledge, New York, 2024.

Campbell, Genevieve (with Tiwi Elders and knowledge holders), *The Old Songs are Always New,* Sydney University Press, Sydney 2023.

Curkpatrick, Samuel, *Singing Bones: Ancestral Creativity and Collaboration*, Sydney University Press, Sydney, 2020.

Curran, Georgia, *Sustaining Indigenous Songs: Contemporary Warlpiri Ceremonial Life in Central Australia*, Berghahn, New York, 2020.

Curran, Georgia, Linda Barwick, Valerie Napaljarri Martin, Simon Japangardi Fisher & Nicolas Peterson (eds), *Vitality and Change in Warlpiri Songs: Juju-ngaliyarlu karnalu-jana pina-pina-manu kurdu-warnu-patu jujuku,* Sydney University Press/Pintubi Anmatjere Warlpiri Media and Communications, Sydney/Yuendumu, 2024.

Dussart, Françoise, *The Politics of Ritual in and Aboriginal Settlement: Kinship, Gender and the Currency of Knowledge*, Smithsonian, Washington, 2000.

Gallagher, Coral Napangardi, Peggy Nampijinpa Brown, Georgia Curran & Barbara Napanangka Martin, *Jardiwanpa yawulyu: Warlpiri women's songs from Yuendumu* (inc. CD), Batchelor Institute, Batchelor, NT, 2014.

Hodgetts, Jesse, *Guthi Girrmara 'Stirring Up Songs' Reawakening Archived Wangaaypuwan and Wiradjuri songs to inform our Culture, Language and Identity*, PhD thesis, University of Newcastle, 2023.

Maatakitj (Clint Bracknell), *Nyoongar Wonderland*, Produced by Paul Mac, Perth, 2022.

Magowan, Fiona & Karl Neuenfelt (eds), *Landscapes of Indigenous Performance: Music, song and dance of the Torres Strait and Arnhem Land*, Aboriginal Studies Press, Canberra, 2005.

Marett, Allan, *Songs, Dreamings and Ghosts: The Wangga of North Australia*. Wesleyan University Press, Middletown, Connecticut, 2006.

Marett, Allan, Linda Barwick & Lysbeth Ford, *For the sake of a song. Wangga songmen and their repertories*, Sydney University Press, Sydney, 2013.

Meakins, Felicity & Myfany Turpin, *Songs from the Stations by Ronnie Wavehill Wirrpnga, Topsy Dodd Ngarnjal and Dandy Danbayarri*, Sydney University Press, Sydney, 2021.

Warlpiri Women from Yuendumu (with Georgia Curran), *Yurntumu-wardingki juju-ngaliya-kurlangu yawulyu: Warlpiri women's songs from Yuendumu* [with four short films on DVD], Batchelor Institute Press, Batchelor, NT, 2017. [Films also available on Indigenous Community Television (ICTV) searching 'yawulyu'].

FILMS

Betz, David, *Singing the Milky Way: a journey into the Dreaming*, 2016.

Lander, Ned & Rachel Perkins, *Jardiwarnpa: A Warlpiri Fire Ceremony*, Film Australia, Sydney,1993.

McKenzie, Kim, *Waiting for Harry*, Australian Institute of Aboriginal Studies, Canberra, 1980.

Sandhall, Roger & Nicolas Peterson, A Warlbiri Fire Ceremony: Ngatjakula, Australian Institute of Aboriginal Studies, Canberra,1977 [1967].

INDEX

Note: Page numbers in **bold** refer to images or captions.

ABOUT THE AUTHORS

Wesley Enoch, AM is a Quandamooka man with over 35 years of working in theatre, events and ceremonies. He is a multi-award-winning playwright and director, and his plays include *The 7 Stages of Grieving* (cowritten with Deborah Mailman), *Cookies Table*, *The Sunshine Club*, *Black Medea*, and more. He has directed groundbreaking shows such as *The Sapphires*, *Black Diggers*, *The Visitors*, and run numerous arts companies including Kooemba Jdarra, Ilbijerri Theatre Company, Queensland Theatre Company, and was Director of the Sydney Festival. Wesley has also created segments for the 2006 and 2018 Commonwealth Games Opening ceremonies. He is currently Deputy Chair of Creative Australia and Professor of Indigenous Practice, Creative Industries at QUT.

Dr Georgia Curran is an anthropologist and ethnomusicologist who has collaborated with Warlpiri people and organisations across the Central Australian Tanami Desert for the last 20 years. She is currently a senior research fellow at the Conservatorium of Music, The University of Sydney. Her publications include *Sustaining Indigenous Songs* (Berghahn, 2020), two-song books – *Jardiwanpa yawulyu* and *Yurntumu-wardingki juju-ngaliya-kurlangu yawulyu: Warlpiri women's songs from Yuendumu* (Batchelor, 2014 and 2017), and an edited collection, Vitality and Change in Warlpiri Songs (Sydney University Press, 2024). Georgia also has broader global interests in minority music traditions, publishing an edited collection on *Supporting Vulnerable Performance Traditions* (Routledge, 2024) and co-producing a podcast *Music!Dance!Culture!*. She is the current Chair of the International Council for Traditions of Music and Dance (ICTMD) Study Group on Music and Dance of Oceania and sits on the advisory board of the Music and Minorities Research Centre, University of Music and Performing Arts Vienna.

Praise for the First Knowledges series …

'This beautiful, important series is a gift and a tool. Use it well.'

—Tara June Winch

'An in-depth understanding of Indigenous expertise and achievement.'

—Quentin Bryce, AD, CVO, FAAL, FASSA

'Australians are yearning for a different approach to land management. Let this series begin the discussion. Let us allow the discussion to develop and deepen.'

—Bruce Pascoe

'These First Knowledges books are proving among the most fascinating and important titles I have ever read; an astounding gift of wisdom delivered with generosity and optimism, offering no less than a new vision of what Australia is, and what it can be … they deserve to change minds, lives, and hopefully the development of Australia itself.'

—Jez Ford

The best of both worlds

TITLES IN THE FIRST KNOWLEDGES SERIES

SONGLINES
Margo Ngawa Neale & Lynne Kelly
(2020)

DESIGN
Alison Page & Paul Memmott
(2021)

COUNTRY
Bill Gammage & Bruce Pascoe
(2021)

ASTRONOMY
Karlie Noon & Krystal De Napoli
(2022)

PLANTS
Zena Cumpston, Michael-Shawn Fletcher & Lesley Head
(2022)

LAW
Marcia Langton & Aaron Corn
(2023)

INNOVATION
Ian J McNiven & Lynette Russell
(2023)

HEALTH
Shawana Andrews, Sandra Eades & Fiona Stanley
(2024)

CEREMONY
Wesley Enoch & Georgia Curran
(2025)

POLITICS
Mary Graham & Morgan Brigg
(2026)

Published in conjunction with the National Museum of Australia
and supported by the Australia Council for the Arts.

FRONT INSIDE COVER: Warlpiri women, Lee Nangala Wayne (front) and Enid Nangala, dance the Pamapardu yawulyu 'flying termite women's ceremonies' for a Southern Ngaliya dance camp at Old Nyirrpi.

BACK INSIDE COVER: Electric Fields – Zaachariaha Fielding and Michael Ross (on keyboard).

From today to tomorrow we dance time. The very old is alive today in many ways.